ALON

WITH GOD

PERSONAL
INTERCESSIONS

By

GROVER CARLTON EMMONS
First Editor of The Upper Room

THE UPPER ROOM
The World's Most Widely Used Devotional Guide
and
Other Devotional Literature
1908 GRAND AVENUE
NASHVILLE 5, TENNESSEE

Second Printing 1953
Third Printing 1955
Fourth Printing 1957
Fifth Printing 1961

UR—19—50—10—1261
Printed in The United States of America

ALONE WITH GOD

PRAYER is that instinctive impulse of the human soul that reaches out after God. It expresses itself in different forms and with varying degrees of distinctiveness which are influenced by the background of one's own experience. With the unenlightened worshipper it may be nothing more than the crude supplications and contortions of heathenism; with others it may be the impulse of a hungry soul in quest of the "unknown God"; with others it may be the effort to know God and to bring themselves into unison with His plans and purposes.

The spirit of effectual prayer is not an effort to supplicate God into changing His will or acting differently from what He would otherwise do. Jesus prayed, "Thy will be done," but He sought to discover and understand that will and align himself with it. Therefore, the seeker after God may well follow the example of the disciple of old and plead, "Lord, teach us to pray."

These prayers have grown out of the experience of a period of years. May they be of assistance to others in giving expression to those deep yearnings of the human soul which become evident when we enter into the presence of God, where all secrets are revealed and we come face to face with reality.

FOREWORD

One day Grover Emmons and I were talking about the devotional life of church members, and I told him I thought there should be a little book of printed prayers for each day of the year, a book for people to use daily. He replied: "I have been working on something of that kind for a long time." He reached in his desk and drew out a folder and showed me hundreds of prayers that he had written from time to time during his busy life. Most of these had been typed by his secretary; some were still in his own handwriting. He wrote those prayers as he sat with his family in the evening, or while waiting in a station for a train or a bus, or even riding on a train or waiting in an office for committees. In his desk at home, many of these prayers were found jotted down in pencil. Some had been written just a few days before his home-going. As the heavenly Father revealed to him a prayer, he wrote it down. The prayers printed in this book came first from the great spiritual nature of Grover Carlton Emmons, as he held communion with his heavenly Father.

After the unexpected death of Dr. Emmons on April 14, 1944, it was determined by The Upper Room to publish the prayers of its founder and first editor. The prayers were then turned over to his wife, Helen K. Emmons, and his editorial assistant, Lucy Gray Kendall, who selected the ones for this volume.

Grover Emmons, as editor of The Upper Room, wrote few meditations for that book, though his deep devotional attitude of mind permeated all its pages. This little book of prayers is reprinted so that the readers of The Upper Room may know the mind, heart, and soul of him whose spiritual life blessed many persons throughout the world. It is our desire that, as the readers of this book use each day these prayers of

A doration
C onfession
T hanksgiving, and
S upplication,

they may become ACTS of God's love, of Christ's redeeming grace, and of the Holy Spirit's power, as was our friend, Grover Carlton Emmons, who walked and talked with God day by day, and who went one day to live in the beautiful garden of eternal prayer.

—Harry Denman
General Secretary,
General Board of Evangelism
Nashville, Tennessee

6

1. O Christ, I dedicate my life anew to Thee at the beginning of this new year. I pray for guidance that every day may be lived on a level that may be worthy of Thy commendation. Direct me by Thy wisdom, sustain me by Thy power, and enable me to serve Thee effectually. I know that I cannot fail if Thou wilt abide with me day by day. In Thy name. Amen.

ॐ ॐ ॐ

2. Heavenly Father, help me to cultivate a sense of Christ's abiding presence. I would be alone with Him in order that His image might be impressed upon my soul and that I might be conformed to His likeness. In this restless age in which we are living, some of us are losing our souls because we do not take time to be alone with Thee. Forbid that I should live as though personal comfort, sensual pleasure, or the acquirement of mere things were life's chief concern or ultimate end. In Christ's name. Amen.

ॐ ॐ ॐ

3. O God, merciful Father, I thank Thee for this new day with all the opportunities it may bring. Give me strength for the work to be done and understanding so that what will have been done when the day is finished may be a worthy gift of service. Amid trials and discouragements, grant that I may be patient and unfaltering. I ask it in the name of the Lord Jesus Christ. Amen.

ॐ ॐ ॐ

4. Gracious Father, Thou art the source of all joy and gladness. May I drink at this fountain today that I may bring joy into the lives of those with whom I walk. Help me to enrich all human relationships by a spirit of good cheer. If disappointment or trial or sorrow comes, may I still rejoice and praise Thee. This is the day which the Lord

has made. I will rejoice and be glad in it, for my Saviour's sake. Amen.

❧ ❧ ❧

5. Heavenly Father, enlighten my understanding and teach me Thy commandments. Give me guidance through Thy Holy Spirit that I may walk in the way of peace. Grant that no gloomy thoughts may shroud my soul or befog my vision. May I have the joy of a redeemed soul; through Jesus Christ my Lord. Amen.

❧ ❧ ❧

6. My God and Father, wilt Thou lead me not into temptation greater than I can bear. Bear me up in Thy hands when trial and testings come, lest they overwhelm me. Give me grace to say, "Thy will, O Lord, be done," for with every temptation Thou dost make a way of escape for my soul. Help me to stand fast in the faith, and to be strong. In the name of my Redeemer. Amen.

❧ ❧ ❧

7. My Father, Thy love is like the ocean. Far out beyond the last horizon there is more and more. Thou didst give Thine only Son to reveal this love to me. Grant that I may grow daily in love, that I may look upon all men with tenderness, and feel Thy compassion for the wounded and the discouraged. Reveal, O God, Thy love in my attitudes, my speech, and my actions. Come and dwell within my soul, Thou Lover of all men, that I may love like Thee. In the name of my blessed Lord. Amen.

❧ ❧ ❧

8. Heavenly Father, it is a sad commentary upon human nature that so many of us have not learned how to live together as human beings. Take from me any narrow view

8

of life and its relationships. As I sit at the feet of Jesus, may I rise above all divisive forces and learn the art of noble living: for Jesus' sake. Amen.

❧ ❧ ❧

9. O Lord, I commit myself to Thee without any reservation. I beseech Thee to cleanse my heart of all stains of sin and give me such a sense of direction that I may avoid all the pitfalls of evil. I ask it in the name of Thy dear Son who died the death of the cross for the redemption of men. Amen.

❧ ❧ ❧

10. O Lord, I crave the consciousness of Thy presence continuously. All else is unsatisfying. My soul is restless until it finds an abiding place in Thee. I seek Thee above all that the mind can conceive. No gift of man or personal attainment sufficeth without Thee. Take from me everything that may make it impossible for me to sense Thy presence; through Jesus Christ the Lord. Amen.

❧ ❧ ❧

11. Gracious Lord, I pray Thee for that guidance through the day that will make me mindful of even the smallest ministries. May I be thoughtful of others, kind in speech, and sympathetic in manner. Give me the Christ-love for men, especially for the lonely, neglected, and needy. May I carry hope to the discouraged, comfort to those in sorrow, and strength to the weak; for Jesus' sake. Amen.

❧ ❧ ❧

12. Merciful God, I am content to trust Thee, for Thou art eternally good. I fear no evil tidings when my heart is fixed on Thee. Sustain me by the power of Thy might and forbid that I should go unfed at the banquet which Thou

hast laid for the children of men. I praise Thee for the abounding riches of Thy grace; through the Lord Jesus Christ. Amen.

❧ ❧ ❧

13. Heavenly Father, give me guidance through this day that my life may find rootage in Christ Jesus my Lord and that my soul may be nurtured by the means of grace so essential to all spiritual development. May I share the sacrificial spirit of Him who voluntarily became the servant of all. May I be so related to Him as the source of spiritual life that I may experience the joy of abundant living. In His name. Amen.

❧ ❧ ❧

14. O God, teach me to love to be alone with Thee, to dwell upon Thee only, that I may be conscious of my need of Thee. May I love the solitude which brings me into perfect fellowship with Thee. May my soul know the sweetness of Thy presence when the world is shut away and I am alone with Thee. Show me Thyself. "Jesus Only" is the cry of my heart. Hear me for the sake of Him who is my Saviour. In Thy dear name. Amen.

❧ ❧ ❧

15. O God, may it be my privilege to view the exalted Christ in all His glory as the reigning Lord and external King. May my faith be so centered in the living Christ that I may experience daily His regenerating power. May I reflect His image, though faint the reflection be, in that circle where my lot may be cast this day. May my life have the poise and strength which comes to those who have been with Jesus. In His name. Amen.

❧ ❧ ❧

16. O Lord, I pray Thee that I may be delivered from sin in all its devious forms. Defend me with Thy mighty

power and grant that all my ways may be ordered of Thee. Give me a courageous heart and strength to overcome every temptation; through Jesus Christ the Lord. Amen.

✤ ✤ ✤

17. O Thou omnipotent One, I bow in reverence before Thee. I am humbled with a sense of littleness in Thy presence. Yet Thou hast given me a sense of kinship with Thee, and Thy dear Son hast taught me to call Thee "Father." I praise Thee, I bless Thee, I adore Thee, O Lord God of hosts. In the name of Christ. Amen.

✤ ✤ ✤

18. Lord Jesus, forgive me for any indifference to the injustices of life around me. Forgive me for any greed or selfishness or lack of a sense of responsibility for those who are unable to stand the strain of it all. May I learn anew of Thee that I am in a very definite sense my brother's keeper. In Thy name. Amen.

✤ ✤ ✤

19. Lord Jesus, Thou couldst have surrounded Thyself with the comforts and luxuries of life and have lived on a plane of ease which so many seem to feel is the chief goal of life. Instead, Thou didst choose for Thy birthplace a bed of straw and for Thy home the fireside of a man of labor and toil. May I learn today the deeper meaning of that saying of Thine: "If any man will come after me, let him deny himself, and take up his cross, and follow me." Amen.

✤ ✤ ✤

20. My Father, may I ever be thankful for the common joys of life, for they are the tokens of Thy love. Because they are familiar, may I never forget to praise Thee. "Bless the Lord, O my soul, and forget not all his benefits." O

11

deliver me from the sin of ingratitude and forgetfulness, and keep ever before me a realization of Thy goodness and mercy. In Christ's name. Amen.

❧ ❧ ❧

21. Heavenly Father, I pray Thee to deliver me from any spirit of bigotry and narrowness that may compass my soul. Teach me the secret of that sympathetic and compassionate spirit of Thine that no narrow prison walls of selfishness may restrict my soul. Give me a spiritual attitude that will enable me to share that abundant life that Jesus came to bring to men, for His name's sake. Amen.

❧ ❧ ❧

22. Teach me, O God, the secret of prayer. My soul craves a deep and vital knowledge of Thee. In striving after Thee in the secret place, may my soul find Thee and be brought into vital touch with Thee. May I experience that close communion with Thee that will give Thee reality in my daily life. Hear my prayer for Jesus' sake. Amen.

❧ ❧ ❧

23. Grant, heavenly Father, that this day may bring with it a deep understanding of Thy love, that wondrous love of Thine that manifested itself in sending Thine only begotten Son into the world for the redemption of men. I would experience that love in the full assurance of sins forgiven. May this be a day made rich with the benediction of Thy love. In Christ's name. Amen.

❧ ❧ ❧

24. My Father, in the hour of trial Thou dost anticipate my need and dost supply it before the want is felt. Thy mercies are unfailing and the depth of Thy love unfathomed. I praise Thee for Thy goodness and glorify Thee for Thy

visitation. Make me strong today in Thy grace, and equal to all that the day may bring. May I be more than conqueror through Him who loves me. For Jesus' sake. Amen.

❧ ❧ ❧

25. Lord Jesus, Thou hast taught that all believing souls derive from Thee spiritual and eternal life. Thou hast revealed a permanency to human personality which death and the grave cannot interrupt. Grant that this assurance may be so real that I may see in death only a progress into richer regions of being. "O death, where is thy sting? O grave, where is thy victory?" "Thanks be to God, who giveth us the victory through our Lord Jesus Christ." Amen.

❧ ❧ ❧

26. I praise Thee, O Lord, for Thy goodness and mercy. I am so forgetful of Thee and so full of unworthy impulses that I feel wholly unworthy of coming to Thee with any petition. I come only because Jesus has died the death of the cross to bring salvation to such as I. "Create in me a clean heart, O God"; for Jesus' sake. Amen.

❧ ❧ ❧

27. Heavenly Father, at the beginning of this new day I take an inventory of my spiritual stock. I find that my yesterdays are not as full of the Christ spirit as I would make this new day. May Jesus be a burning light in my soul today. May the joy of knowing Him as my Saviour and Redeemer be deeper today than it was yesterday. In His name. Amen.

❧ ❧ ❧

28. Great are thy tender mercies, O Lord! May I never lose sight of those mercies amid the burdens and duties and discouragements of this day. May the remembrance of them

lift me to hope when I am tempted to despair, may they bring peace when I am tempted to be restless, and may they fill my soul with gratitude when I am tempted to be ungrateful. In Christ's name. Amen.

❧ ❧ ❧

29. Bless the Lord, O my soul, and forget not all His benefits. All nature praises Thee. The mighty works of Thy hands unite to sing Thy praise. I, too, would join the chorus of swelling harmonies which laud and magnify Thy glorious name. Thou hast created me to sing Thy praise. As long as I have breath, I will glorify Thy name. I will sing praises unto the Lord forever and ever. Amen.

❧ ❧ ❧

30. O God, may that peace which no earthly disturbance can mar calm my heart amid the troubles and burdens of life. May I have the assurance that my daily walk is in keeping with Thy holy will and may each step bring me into more intimate touch with Thee. May my soul sense Thy approving smile because of the Christ-spirit reflected in my attitudes and contacts with others. In Christ's name. Amen.

❧ ❧ ❧

31. Merciful Father, in the quiet hour of this day and alone with Thee, I confess my sins. I hate them and am humiliated to acknowledge them. My humiliation would be more than I could bear but for Thy mercy and love. O God, forgive my sins, the sins of my body and the sins of my soul, sins committed secretly and sins committed openly. I claim Thy forgiveness in the name of Jesus, who died the death of the cross for sinful men. Amen.

1. O God, I begin this day seeking Thy leadership and direction. There are duties to be faced today in which I shall need Thy help and guidance. There are temptations coming across my path which will be too much for me unless I am fully conscious of Thy presence. May my choices and decisions through the day be determined by a deep sense of spiritual values. May my life be kept toned by a sense of the presence of the Holy Spirit. Amen.

❧ ❧ ❧

2. Dear Lord, I pray for an utter renunciation of self, a complete obedience to Thy holy will. No partial giving of myself will suffice. Nothing less than complete surrender will satisfy myself or Thee. May my soul be sensitive to the faintest whisper of Thy voice. May I love to do Thy will. Let me know the sweet joys of completely resigning my whole life to Thee. In Thy name and for Thy sake. Amen.

❧ ❧ ❧

3. O Lord, keep me from bitterness today. May no harsh or unkind thoughts find an abiding place in my heart. Defend me against the weakness of self-pity. Enable me to attain holiness of life, and may Thy power encompass me and enable me to walk in paths of peace. In the blessed Redeemer's name. Amen.

❧ ❧ ❧

4. Heavenly Father, I am mindful of the fact that Thou dost need consecrated lives through whom Thou canst express Thyself in the affairs of the world. May I abide in Christ and have such deep union with Him that I may bear much fruit for Thee. Give me daily guidance and spiritual enrichment; through Jesus Christ the Lord. Amen.

5. O God, who art the fountain of all wisdom and in whom all power dwelleth, create in me a desire to learn of Thee. Make me eager for knowledge of Thyself, for an understanding of Thy nature, and Thy laws, and Thy dealings with men. May I be able to fix my thoughts upon Thee that Thou mayest impart Thyself to me. May there be a great expectancy within my heart. May I see Thee in all of life and love Thy appearing; for Christ's sake. Amen.

❧ ❧ ❧

6. O Lord, lead Thy people in the task of making Thy love known to all the world. Thou hast created of one blood all nations, and it must grieve Thee that Thy children have fallen so far short of Thy expectations in making Thy love known to all men. May I be endued with power this day that will enable me to meet my share of this responsibility and effectually bear witness to the wondrous love of God in Christ. Amen.

❧ ❧ ❧

7. O Christ, teach me Thy way. Help me to reflect Thy gentleness in all the events of life, Thy compassion for those who suffer, Thy care for those who fear, Thy redemptive love for those in sin. May life be full of power for good as I face my daily responsibilities. In Christ's blessed name I pray. Amen.

❧ ❧ ❧

8. O blessed Father, I would know the blessing which comes from the discipline of life. I would come into sonship through the experience of chastening at Thy hand, knowing that from under its rod I shall arise cleansed, forgiven, purer, wiser, and stronger to face the future. Through suffering may my soul grow in gentleness and in understanding; and in submission to Thy will may I attain unto

maturity of character; for the sake of my Lord and Saviour Jesus Christ. Amen.

❧   ❧   ❧

9. Heavenly Father, I give Thee thanks for the gift of Thy Son, and the revelation of Thyself which He has given to the world. Through Him I have come to know Thee in the fullness of Thy love and mercy. Through Him I have a knowledge of Thy compassion for suffering humanity and the yearning of Thy father-heart for fellowship with Thy children. Amen.

❧   ❧   ❧

10. Eternal God, I thank Thee for the Christian way of life and pray that Thou wilt give me guidance to walk daily in that way with unfaltering step. It is a way that has been beaten hard by the footsteps of saints and martyrs down through the centuries. May I be worthy of the heritage that has come to me through them, and never grow weary or discouraged as along the way I go. In Christ's name. Amen.

❧   ❧   ❧

11. O Christ, who didst calm the tossing billows of the sea, speak peace to my troubled soul. Let me find beneath the sorrows of this life that deep eternal calm which lies beneath the surface storms and goes deep into the lower waters. Thou art the Master of my spirit. Speak to me, Lord, that I may rest in Thee; for Thy name's sake. Amen.

❧   ❧   ❧

12. My Father, the vicissitudes of this life are like the ceaseless tides of the sea, forever changing in their ebb and flow. Only one anchor holds amid the changing years. O Thou who changest not, leave me not alone. Uphold me with the everlasting arms, that my heart fail not and my

faith be sure and steadfast. Thou art my Rock. In the blessed name of my Lord, I pray. Amen.

♪ ♪ ♪

13. O God, Father of all, may the dissensions which divide Thy children disappear; bring all men into the unity of love; may peace and good will prevail. May Thy children in all lands be so definitely conscious of their unity in Thee that mutual helpfulness may become a reality; through the grace, mercy, and tenderness of Thy Son, Jesus Christ. Amen.

♪ ♪ ♪

14. Heavenly Father, when life seems long and hard, reach out Thy hand to help me and keep me from falling. In a tempestuous sea Thou art as a mighty rock to which I may cling and find security. Uphold me by the power of Thy might, I ask in the name of Jesus Christ, my Lord and Saviour. Amen.

♪ ♪ ♪

15. Merciful God, forgive me, I beseech Thee, for the sins I have committed against Thee. Deliver me when I am tempted and incline my heart to do Thy will. Free me from pride, envy, selfishness, covetousness—from all those things that dwarf life. Grant me at all times the support of Thy presence; and for any achievement I may attain, I will give Thee the praise, through Jesus Christ the Lord. Amen.

♪ ♪ ♪

16. O Lord God Almighty, I pray Thee to look with compassionate heart upon those on whom have fallen the miseries of war. Be present with the wounded and dying and comfort the broken-hearted with the touch of Thy hand. In all the gloom and sorrow of the world help me

to be patient when the night-watch seems long, and may my face ever be toward the eastern sky where day breaketh and the sun of righteousness doth glow. In the name of Him who is our peace. Amen.

* * *

17. O my Father, from days of testing and affliction, give me the power to take hold of life anew, that out of weariness and sorrow and tribulation I may bear a strong and valiant spirit. Help me to grasp Thy eternal hand, and face the future unafraid. With Thee there is grace for even my greatest need. Thy mercy still holds me fast. To Thy name be all the praise forever. Amen.

* * *

18. Almighty God, Maker of all things and Judge of all men, I come into Thy presence with penitent heart and earnestly repent of the sins which I have committed by thought, word, and deed against Thee. Have mercy upon me, holy Father, and forgive all my misdoings and help me so to live each day as to please Thee. In Christ's blessed name. Amen.

* * *

19. O merciful Father, who hast promised forgiveness of sins to all who come to Thee with penitent hearts, I come now trusting in Thy promises and ask for Thy pardon and for deliverance from the burden of my sins. Give me that blessed peace of heart and confirm and strengthen me in all goodness; through Jesus Christ the Lord. Amen.

* * *

20. Almighty and eternal God, because Thou hast promised through Thine only begotten Son, saying, "Ask, and it shall be given you; seek, and ye shall find; knock, and it shall be opened unto you," I come with an earnest plea

for the forgiveness of my sins and that Thou wilt open unto me through the guidance of the Holy Spirit the way that leads to the abundant life. In Christ's name. Amen.

❧ ❧ ❧

21. My heavenly Father, give me a vision of goodness, beauty, and truth, and grant me the grace to obey the vision. May I have a passion and desire to lift life out of the sordid up to the flame of high and holy endeavor. Give me the mind of Jesus and inspire me with a purpose to be more like Him. In His blessed name. Amen.

❧ ❧ ❧

22. O God, who dost ever seek to guide men aright, teach me the simple path of obedience. Enable me to live each day under the inspiration of Thy Word and in the daily realization of Thy abiding presence. Give me richly of Thy love and grace that I may be kind in my speech and actions, and may I be graciously sympathetic and brotherly in all my attitudes. I ask in the name of Jesus Christ our Lord. Amen.

❧ ❧ ❧

23. Our Father who art in heaven, I thank Thee for the opportunities of this day. Sanctify my toil with Thy presence until all my work shall have been transformed into worship; and may my worship find expression in helpful service. Strengthen me, I beseech Thee, so that I may stand every test and withstand every unworthy temptation. May I endure as seeing Him who is invisible. In the name of Him who is the strength of my life. Amen.

❧ ❧ ❧

24. O Lord, my God, help me to realize that my task is to do the work Thou hast given me to do. May I not merely refrain from doing evil, but may I seek to do for my

fellow men some service beyond that required or expected of me. Realize Thy purpose in me, through Christ our Redeemer. Amen.

❧ ❧ ❧

25. Almighty God, who, according to the multitude of Thy mercies, dost forgive the sins of those who truly repent, have mercy upon me, for I earnestly desire pardon and forgiveness. Renew in me whatsoever has been taken away by sin and strengthen Thy servant with Thy blessed Spirit, through the merits of Jesus Christ our Lord. Amen.

❧ ❧ ❧

26. Blessed Holy Spirit, I thank Thee that Thou canst change my heart and renew a right spirit within me. Thou canst take away all hate and harshness and impatience and evil thinking, and replace them with all heavenly virtues, love, gentleness, peace, and joy. Only Thou art able to do this for me. I am helpless without Thee, O Lord. Oh live Thou within me, now and evermore, for Thy name's glory and to Thy praise. Amen.

❧ ❧ ❧

27. O Lord, I pray Thee to guide me in the right use of the talent which Thou hast committed to me. May I be a worthy servant in its use and at the end be able to render a good account of my stewardship. May each day of my life be treasured as a precious gem and used as a gift from my God. In Christ's name. Amen.

❧ ❧ ❧

28. Heavenly Father, I crave a deeper experience of Thee. I seem at times so out of touch with Thee that there is an emptiness in my soul like a great void. Give me an abiding consciousness of Thy presence and may my innermost being be sustained by Thy presence, for Jesus' sake. Amen.

1. O God, I kneel before Thee in this new dawn. Thou hast refreshed my body with the rest of the night, and my spirit with the dews of Thy peace. Gird me with Thy wisdom to live wisely and guide me in the ways of service for Thee. Throughout this day I would never lose Thy hand. Bind my heart to Thee with ties of heavenly friendship, and may overflowing joy be my portion; through Jesus Christ my Lord. Amen.

❧ ❧ ❧

2. Heavenly Father, help me this day to translate my creed into life. May my life be so dominated by the Master that it may reflect the light of Him who is the Light of the World. If I should contact a discouraged soul, grant that that contact may bring the inspiration of a new hope. May I live my life this day so as to help some burdened soul to lighten his load. Amen.

❧ ❧ ❧

3. O God, help me to crown this new day with the beauty of having done Thy will. Help me to meet the tasks of the day by giving me an understanding of all Thou wouldst have me do. I give myself anew to Thee and shall ever seek to realize Thy purposes as Thy will is made known. I covet no riches, but seek the riches of a life that is at-one-ment with Thee. Amen.

❧ ❧ ❧

4. O Thou, who art my refuge and strength, I open the door of my heart to Thee. Help me to keep my spirit high and give me courage to hold to the truth as revealed in Jesus Christ Thy Son. Guide me in the development of poise amid this world's clamor and endue me with the serenity of those who trust in Thy unfailing presence. Teach me to walk with Thee and so gain the best that life can bring to me and to others. In Christ's name. Amen.

5. O Thou King eternal, teach me how to take up my cross and follow Thee. Enable me to count each responsibility, each task, each cross, as a stewardship from Thee. Help me to impart something of the radiance of Christ to others. Help me not to rebel when the burdens of life weigh down upon me, remembering always that the great Burden-bearer walks beside me and understands it all. In His name. Amen.

❧ ❧ ❧

6. O God, grant me eyes to see the glory that crowns a life of unselfish devotion to Thee. Cleanse my emotions, purify my soul, and give depth to my life. Breathe into me the breath of eternal life and may I go to my tasks each day with the assurance of those who possess immortality. I pray in the name of Jesus Christ my Lord. Amen.

❧ ❧ ❧

7. O Lord, who in Thy days upon this earth didst yearn and seek for evidences of faith in the hearts of men, increase within my own heart a great and unshakable faith. So fill my heart with trust in Thee that I may never doubt the final triumph of Thy purpose for this world. May I know a great calm within my spirit because I believe in the ultimate victory of Thy Kingdom. Despair and confusion will yield at last to Thy will, and Thy dream for mankind shall be accomplished. To this end use all my life and powers; for the sake of Him who died to redeem a lost world. Amen.

❧ ❧ ❧

8. I thank thee, holy Father, for the gift of life, for the beautiful things life brings to me each day, and for life abundant in Christ Jesus. To Thee I dedicate myself and all that I have. Guide me in my daily walk to the end that I may be worthy to be called Thy child. In Christ's blessed name. Amen.

9. Holy Father, I pray that I may not let my religion be "a thing of selfish ecstasy," but rather let me share it with tender love for all mankind. Today let me find one burdened, lonely heart and open for it the shining portals to that heavenly life with Thee, wherein my own soul delights to dwell; for the sake of my blessed Saviour. Amen.

❧ ❧ ❧

10. O Christ, the world's supreme Burden-bearer, sustain me when I face hardship and tribulation that I may not falter or fall. Discipline me, as Thou seest best, and make me strong by the power of Thy might. Teach me self-mastery, and enable me to press on toward that perfection exemplified by Thee. In Thy name. Amen.

❧ ❧ ❧

11. My Father, help me to face the future with eager eyes and with a fearless heart. May my gaze be forever upward and onward welcoming new discoveries of Thy truth and new revelations of Thy purposes for the world. May I grasp the fingers of the past only as they guide me to a richer, fuller life ahead. In the name of my Master. Amen.

❧ ❧ ❧

12. Heavenly Father, I have failed Thee so often that I must come to Thee, in meekness and sorrow, to plead for Thy forgiveness. Out of the abundance of Thy love have compassion on me and forgive my wicked ways. Amen.

❧ ❧ ❧

13. Lord Jesus, make my heart Thy dwelling place. Grant that it may be emptied of self and sin. Help me to be true to Thee and may Thy purposes be realized in my daily walk. May Thy presence so possess me that I may be able to say with the apostle: "For to me to live is Christ." Amen.

14. O God, give me a deeper understanding of Thy truth, and may I fathom the inner meaning of the Christian life. In a very real way may "I press toward the mark for the prize of the high calling of God in Christ Jesus." "Amid th' encircling gloom" of a world of sin, suffering, and sorrow, "lead Thou me on!" In Christ's name. Amen.

※ ※ ※

15. Merciful God, lift me into the pure light of Thy presence that I may walk through the confusion of these tragic days unafraid. Even though the foundations be shaken, I will fear no evil if Thou art with me. Enable me to think and to act in obedience to Thy holy will. Amen.

※ ※ ※

16. Heavenly Father, amid the noise and distractions in the world around me, I would enjoy a sacred tryst with Thee. When I shut the doors of my soul to be alone with Thee, I find strength for service and aid for victorious living. Give me that inner peace and power through Christ. Amen.

※ ※ ※

17. Holy Spirit of God, may I heed within my heart Thy promptings of love and truth which will show me my darkness and lead me to true repentance. Make me sensitive to Thy voice, and inspire me continually to seek Thy guidance in my earthly life. Guide me into all truth and lead me into a life of complete obedience to my Lord. Amen.

※ ※ ※

18. Heavenly Father, support me this day under all the difficulties I shall face and make Thy way plain unto me. I need Thy sustaining grace every day. Out of the fullness of Thy wisdom and understanding, minister unto my frailities that I may be equal to all demands upon me. For Jesus' sake. Amen.

19. O God I praise Thee for Thy unfailing ministry to my daily needs. Thy care is unremitting, Thy saving power is always available, Thy love is daily revealed, Thy mercy is ever apparent. Help me to be worthy of Thee and may no deed of mine ever cast reproach upon Thy holy name. In Christ's name. Amen.

⚜ ⚜ ⚜

20. Heavenly Father, guide me this day into right choices. May my spiritual vision become clarified as I think upon things that are true, just, pure, and lovely. Work Thou effectively in my soul and satisfy its longing for spiritual enrichment. May my walk with Thee bring peace of mind and contentment of heart. In Christ's name I pray. Amen.

⚜ ⚜ ⚜

21. O God, amid the evil with which I am surrounded, I do not pray for a way of escape from temptation; but I pray that Thou wilt give me strength and courage to overcome temptation. I would not seek seclusion from life's testings; I would be made strong through a vital faith in order that I may withstand them. In Christ's name. Amen.

⚜ ⚜ ⚜

22. O God, as the hart panteth after the water brooks, so panteth my soul for Thee, the fount of living water. Let me daily drink of those waters that my spiritual thirst may be satisfied and that all that is within me may rejoice in Thy salvation. Nothing apart from Thee can satisfy the longings of my soul nor sustain me in the hour of need. In Christ's name I pray. Amen.

⚜ ⚜ ⚜

23. O God, let the light of Thy love shine forth in the dark and dreary places of life where I may be called to walk.

In the radiance of that light, I walk with no uncertain step. Direct me in all my doings that I may glorify Thy holy name, and finally by Thy mercy obtain everlasting life; through Jesus Christ the Lord. Amen.

❧ ❧ ❧

24. Heavenly Father, in a world in which there is so much brutal destruction and unwarranted aggression, may I never fail to discern and visualize a world fashioned after the mind of Jesus Christ, a world worthy of Him who died upon a cross to redeem it. Empower me, O God, that I may do my part worthily toward making that kind of a world a reality. Through Jesus Christ the Lord. Amen.

❧ ❧ ❧

25. Heavenly Father, there are many times when I am puzzled and unable to understand why Thou dost permit some things to happen in this world of Thine. And yet, I know that Thou art too wise to make a mistake and too good to do a wrong. May this knowledge save me from any spirit of rebelliousness and hold me steady when the foundations seem unsteady. Through Jesus Christ my Lord. Amen.

❧ ❧ ❧

26. Heavenly Father, when the lengthening shadows fall athwart my way, may I lift my eyes to behold the light of Thy face. May I be ever conscious of Thy presence and the availability of Thy help. When Thou art near, I will fear no evil. Undergird me with Thy love and sustain me in all times of testing. In Christ's name I pray. Amen.

❧ ❧ ❧

27. O God, I thank Thee for Thy fatherly goodness. Amid the sorrow and suffering and tragedy of the world, it is comforting to know that Thou dost not withhold Thy

love from the broken-hearted. Open the doors of a new life to a suffering and spiritually hungry generation. May a better day dawn in which "All the ends of the earth shall see the salvation of our God"; through Christ the Lord. Amen.

🌿 🌿 🌿

28. O God, teach me to have that faith in Thee that knows no defeat, that faith that has sustained heroic souls in days of old. Thou art the same loving Father as in ages past and just as ready to make available Thy redemptive power to those who love and serve Thee. May I daily fight the good fight of faith; through Christ my Saviour. Amen.

🌿 🌿 🌿

29. My Father, Thou art very near. Thou art with him who is of a contrite and humble spirit. I have seen Thy face in the face of Thy Son, Jesus Christ; I have heard Thy voice in the words of my blessed Saviour; I have seen Thy works in the deeds of the gentle Jesus. Thy heart is made known to me in the death of my Lord. My Father, I offer to Thee the utter love of my heart forever. In His name. Amen.

🌿 🌿 🌿

30. Heavenly Father, as I go through life meeting the routine of each day, I feel the need of Thee. There is a feeling of inadequacy and a sense of need which Thou alone canst fill. Give me guidance and strength and understanding, that I may meet Thy expectations. For Christ's sake. Amen.

🌿 🌿 🌿

31. Heavenly Father, I thank Thee for every provision Thou hast made for the enrichment of the spiritual life of Thy children. Through the reading of Thy Holy Word and through fellowship with Thee in prayer, may I grow strong in my inner life and enjoy that enrichment that is attained through knowledge of the Lord Jesus Christ. Amen.

1. O living Christ, may I be empowered by a consciousness of immortality. Thou didst say to Thy disciples of old: "Because I live, ye shall live also." May I know the lifting power of that promise in my daily walk. Amen.

※ ※ ※

2. My Saviour, Thy Cross is ever before me. There I see Thy dying form lifted for my redemption, and my soul is lost in wonder and in adoring love. Thou hast given Thyself for me, and in return I give Thee the utter love of my heart. O accept this obligation of myself that I may be forever Thine; for Thy name's sake I pray. Amen.

※ ※ ※

3. O God, I thank Thee for the gift of Thine only begotten Son, who came to live and die and rise again that men might be saved. In Him I find a revelation of Thy wondrous love, and, in accepting Him as my Saviour, I come under the dominion of Thy will. Unto Thee I render praise for the heritage I have in Christ Jesus. Amen.

※ ※ ※

4. Heavenly Father, I thank Thee for the stamp of divine approval which Thou hast placed upon the claims and ministry of Jesus Christ by raising Him from the dead. Oh, how this assurance is needed as I come face to face with my sins! He has promised forgiveness and, through the seal of Thy approval, I have the assurance that my faith in Him has not been misplaced. I thank Thee in the name of Jesus Christ, the Lord and Master. Amen.

※ ※ ※

5. Heavenly Father, I thank Thee for the living hope Thou hast given to the world through the resurrection of Jesus Christ from the dead. On the morning of His resur-

rection, as He came forth from the tomb, there was ushered in a new and better day for the world. How the world needs a rebirth of this resurrection hope! May Thy people everywhere commit themselves to Jesus and His way of life, for under the sway of that hope we are equipped for the building of a better world wherein dwelleth righteousness and peace. In Christ's name. Amen.

❧ ❧ ❧

6. Heavenly Father, may the splendor of the resurrected life be mine today. May I walk in companionship with my risen Lord. May old sins, old failures, old sorrows be forgotten, and a new life begun. Thou hast forgiven the past. Thou art my living Lord, the source of all power and strength. I rejoice in Thee and consecrate my life anew this day; for Christ's sake. Amen.

❧ ❧ ❧

7. Lord, I thank Thee for Thy goodness and love. Surely Thou art merciful and kind in Thy dealings with those who are Thy very own. At times Thou dost seem to move in mysterious ways Thy wonders to perform, but underneath and motivating all is a plan and purpose saturated with love that is infinite. May a deeper knowledge and understanding of that love enrich my life and lead me to spiritual heights where my vision of Thee shall be unobstructed. In Jesus' name. Amen.

❧ ❧ ❧

8. My heavenly Father, help me to bear suffering nobly, knowing that in so doing I may work with Thee in the holy task of redeeming Thy world. May my pain refine my character, deepen my compassion for others, and inspire those who may be watching my life. In my deepest suffering may I remember the greatest sufferer, Thy beloved Son,

who bore earth's greatest suffering on Calvary's cross. In the name of my blessed Lord. Amen.

❧ ❧ ❧

9. Guide me, O Lord, with the light of life that I may not stumble through the darkness of a meaningless and profitless existence. Grant that I may have such a vision of the abiding worth of the things of God that no personal inconvenience or hard circumstances may cause me to falter or refuse to go where duty calls. For Jesus' sake. Amen.

❧ ❧ ❧

10. O gracious Lord, I love Thee because Thou hast said, "I am the resurrection, and the life." When I stand beside the open grave with breaking heart, I can look beyond its agony and hear Thy voice, "Because I live, ye shall live also." May this assurance be mine every day. In Thy name I pray. Amen.

❧ ❧ ❧

11. O Lord, I bow in adoration before Thee, the all-wise architect of this universe. "In the beginning hast thou laid the foundations of the earth; and the heavens are the works of thine hands." The rolling hills and majestic mountains, the skies like a canopy adorned with ten thousand jewels more precious than diamonds or sapphires, nature everywhere thrills my soul with a deep sense of Thy wisdom and love. "Sing, O ye heavens; for the Lord hath done it: shout, ye lower parts of the earth: break forth into singing, ye mountains, O forest, and every tree therein." Unto Thee be all glory forever. In Christ's name. Amen.

❧ ❧ ❧

12. Heavenly Father, I come before Thee with penitent heart and pray for the forgiveness of my sins. I would turn my back upon the ways of sin and walk with Christ in the

ways of righteousness. Enable me, O God, to bear the fruit of repentance, faith, and holiness of life; through Jesus Christ my Saviour. Amen.

❧ ❧ ❧

13. Heavenly Father, this day I would remember before Thy throne those who are dearest to me. May Thy never-failing love and care be over them, and wilt Thou do for them those things which Thou alone seest that they need. Grant that they may rejoice in Thy service today, and when eventide comes may they rest in Thy peace; through Jesus Christ our Lord. Amen.

❧ ❧ ❧

14. Heavenly Father, give me the spirit of humility and freedom from the spirit of self-seeking in Thy Kingdom. May it be enough to hope that ultimately I shall be blessed in my own life through spiritual growth and enrichment of life for being kind and gracious and helpful to those in need. Let the light of eternity fall upon my daily path. May I do all things with the consciousness that some day I shall stand before Thee. In Christ's name. Amen.

❧ ❧ ❧

15. Blessed Christ, who didst come into the world that men might have life and that they might have it more abundantly, I offer Thee my life that Thou mayest impart to it beauty and richness and buoyancy. Thou alone canst add meaning and enrichment to life above the best that the world has to offer. For Thy name's sake. Amen.

❧ ❧ ❧

16. Eternal God, I praise Thee for the many evidences of Thy mercy and goodness. Grant that I may this day get a new insight into the meaning and purpose of life. Girded with that understanding, may I move a bit closer toward

the attainment of life's goal and enjoy the fullness of living that is the gift of Christ. In His blessed name. Amen.

❧ ❧ ❧

17. O God of grace, grant that through Thy unmerited love toward sinful men in the gift of Thine own dear Son I may come into a deeper knowledge of Thy love, and into a more blessed life of communion with Thee. To Thee I lift up my heart with all its hopes and weaknesses and pray that through bonds of sympathy and unity of purpose Thy will may become the very law of my being; for Jesus' sake. Amen.

❧ ❧ ❧

18. O Christ, Thou art more than the Messiah of a chosen few; Thou art the Saviour of the world. Blessed be Thy name! Equip me in heart and mind to bear effectual witness for Thee by word of mouth and manner of life. May my faith in Thee be so real that it may carry contagion with it and awaken in others a hunger and thirst for Thee. In Thy name and for Thy sake I ask it. Amen.

❧ ❧ ❧

19. O Christ, as I come into the presence of Calvary's Cross, and behold Thee thereon, I am humbled with a sense of unworthiness. In Thine eyes, so full of anguish, I behold infinite love. In Thine arms, outstretched, and in Thy body, torn and pierced, I behold the way of redemption. Above the taunts of Thy tormenters, I hear the echo of the garden of prayer: "Not my will, but thine be done"—even though it lead to a cross. May I be worthy of such a Saviour. Amen.

❧ ❧ ❧

20. O God of all grace and comfort, I thank Thee for the words, "Blessed are they that mourn: for they shall be comforted," for I know that none of Thy promises shall

ever fail. In Thine own good time Thou wilt bring hope and peace to my heart. Never wilt Thou forsake me, though the darkness tarry long, and the dawn come late. I will lift my eyes to Thee, for Thou art my Redeemer and my God. In Christ's dear name. Amen.

❀ ❀ ❀

21. O God of holiness, open my eyes to see that pain and grief can work within my soul ultimate good and lasting reward which can come no other way. May I not shun the lonely way of sorrow and loss, but with my hand in Thine tread it boldly and unafraid, knowing that it will but lead me into a clearer vision of life's meaning and purpose, and find at last the shining of Thy face. For Thy name's sake. Amen.

❀ ❀ ❀

22. Heavenly Father, Thou knowest what things I have need of before I ask them. Therefore, I enter into Thy presence with an assurance of understanding and sympathy. Sustain me in time of need and comfort my affliction out of the fullness of Thy mercy. Take my hand, O Lord, and lead me over every devious path, and I pray Thee, uphold me in time of weakness. In Christ's name I pray. Amen.

❀ ❀ ❀

23. O Christ, Son of God, I am thankful to Thee for the message of hope and salvation which Thou hast brought to the world. When my soul is hungry, Thou givest it the Bread that cometh down from heaven. In Thee, I have peace and gladness of soul, light for the understanding, cleansing for the conscience, and a goal for the loftiest flight of my hopes. With all who adore Thee, I will praise Thy name for ever and ever. Amen.

❀ ❀ ❀

24. Heavenly Father, I would be an obedient subject of Thy Kingdom. Forgive my sins and help me as I seek

holiness of life. Under the guidance of Thy Spirit may I pursue the way that leads to eternal life in Christ Jesus. Give me Thy peace and the joy of the redeemed. In Christ's name. Amen.

❧ ❧ ❧

25. Heavenly Father, I stand in Thy presence as a penitent sinner and claim Thy forgiveness through Jesus Christ, Thy Son. May my sins be cast into the depths of the sea. It is not because of any merit of mine that I claim Thy forgiveness, but I come because of the merit of Thy dear Son whose sacrifice on Calvary avails for even me. Hear my prayer for His sake. Amen.

❧ ❧ ❧

26. Heavenly Father, forbid that I should be satisfied with the husks that the world offers—small things, transitory things, material things—the things for which so many greedily grasp. Feed my soul upon the Bread of Life and help me to seek day by day the riches of Thy grace, through Jesus Christ my Lord. Amen.

❧ ❧ ❧

27. I thank Thee, O God, for the gospel of hope that Thou hast sent to the world through Thy Son, for the assurance that Thou dost really love men and art eager to redeem them from their bondage and their hopelessness and their misery. O Thou great Shepherd of my soul, Thou hast manifested Thy divine solicitude through pain and tears and blood, and hast redeemed my soul. For Thy name's sake, I praise Thee and give Thee the gratitude of my heart. Amen.

❧ ❧ ❧

28. O God, teach me the secret of a life separated from those things which are sinful in Thy sight. Grant that my

life may be filled with acts, purposes, and desires worthy of a child of Thine. May I live an abundant life, a life so wholly taken up with the things that Thou dost approve that evil may find no lodging-place within me. Hear my prayer, for Jesus' sake. Amen.

ℵ ℵ ℵ

29. O Lamb of God, who wast slain before the founda-of the world for my sin, wilt Thou wash the garments of my life that they may be fit clothing for my spirit as it ministers before Thy holy altar. May no unworthy thing be found on them. I would walk before Thee in priestly robes without spot or blemish. O make me pure, for Thy name's sake. Amen.

ℵ ℵ ℵ

30. I thank Thee, O God, for the promise of victory over death and the grave. In this hope the believer may say, "O death, where is thy sting? O grave, where is thy victory?" May I live daily in this hope, and in the end be a partaker of eternal life. May there still be a doxology upon my lips in life's darkest hour. In the name of Jesus Christ our Lord, I ask it. Amen.

1. My Father, in the shadows of the waning night before the dawn breaks anew upon the sleeping world, my spirit flies upward to Thy throne. O my Father, I love to worship Thee! Holy, holy, holy, heaven and earth are full of Thy glory! Glory be to Thee, O Lord most high! Rise anew within my heart, Thou Day Spring from on high! Cleanse anew the fountains of my life and make me pure. I wait before Thee. In Christ's name I pray. Amen.

꙳ ꙳ ꙳

2. O Christ, I thank Thee for the new life Thou hast made possible for me through Thy sacrifices on the cross. Grant that my life in Thee, like the salt to which Thou hast likened it, may be a retarding influence against all the evil around me. Give me holiness of life and use me this day for the advancement of Thy Kingdom, and Thine shall be the glory. Amen.

꙳ ꙳ ꙳

3. Heavenly Father, I thank Thee for Thy concern in regard to everything that pertains to my life. So many things confront me day by day that nobody knows of or even cares about, and sometimes I feel so alone. Yet, with the assurance that not even a sparrow falleth unnoticed by Thee, I am sustained and comforted in my moments of solitude that I have a friend in Thee. For this and all tokens of Thy love, I thank Thee. In Christ's name. Amen.

꙳ ꙳ ꙳

4. Heavenly Father, deliver me from the confusion so prevalent in the world. Grant that my soul may not grope in darkness. Lift me by Thy presence and enable me to walk through these tragic days unafraid. May I have an assurance that is so real that I may truly say, with Thy servant of old, "I know whom I have believed, and am per-

suaded that he is able to keep that which I have committed unto him against that day." In His name. Amen.

      ❧   ❧   ❧

5. Heavenly Father, may I have a sacred tryst with Thee throughout this day. In the midst of all the distractions of the day, grant that I may never lose sight of Thee. Enrich my life by Thy presence, and shelter my soul as it abides in the secret place of the most High. Hear my prayer, for Jesus' sake. Amen.

      ❧   ❧   ❧

6. O God, give me singleness of purpose that I may "press toward the mark for the prize of the high calling of God in Christ Jesus." My life-aim is the formation of a holy character through faith in Him and I pray that nothing may ever subordinate that aim. Grant me grace to be brave enough this day to think and act in obedience to Thy will. In Christ's name. Amen.

      ❧   ❧   ❧

7. Almighty God, wilt Thou cleanse me from secret faults. There are sins deep within my heart which I do not recognize and cannot bring into the light. May Thy revealing light disclose my guilt that I may lay it before Thee, begging forgiveness in the name of my blessed Lord and Saviour Jesus Christ, who died for my redemption. Amen.

      ❧   ❧   ❧

8. Heavenly Father, give me an understanding of Thy eternal laws, and grant that through obedience to them I may build a foundation which will be able to endure the storms and temptations of life. Grant, I beseech Thee, that my daily conduct may be in complete conformity to Thy holy will; through the Lord Jesus Christ. Amen.

9. O God, grant that my life may be fruitful soil for the growth of the good seed Thou dost sow. Forbid that the cares of this life or the pleasures of the world may ever displace Thee in my daily walk. Nurture every good impulse in my life, that it may be fruitful in righteousness. Amen.

❧ ❧ ❧

10. O Lord, I thank Thee for Thy promise to be with Thy children in time of trouble. Today, men everywhere need the comfort of Thy presence. In all the confusion and turmoil and sorrow of this world, I would lose heart if it were not for the blessed assurance that Thou art in the midst of it all. Be Thou my strength and comfort. Amen.

❧ ❧ ❧

11. My Father, there are burdens today too heavy for me to bear without Thee. Let me be aware that Thou didst never intend that I should bear them alone. Grant that I may cast my burdens upon Thee, for then shall I renew my strength, and I shall run and not be weary. O Thou great Burden-bearer of the race, take from my heart this weight of care and give rest unto my soul. In His name. Amen.

❧ ❧ ❧

12. Merciful God, I shudder to think what I might have been, except for Thy gracious providence. Forbid that any pride of personal achievement in righteousness should ever mar my soul. Keep me humble and sympathetic with others who may be struggling against some handicap that makes the going hard. In Christ's name. Amen.

❧ ❧ ❧

13. O God, heaven and earth declare Thy glory; every living thing proclaims Thy might, greatness, and wisdom. Nothing is beyond Thy power; naught can be hid from Thee. In Thy presence I stand with humility, but thankful for the privilege of worshiping Thee; through Christ. Amen.

14. O God, amid the confusion and disorder which sin has brought into the world, I thank Thee for the assurance that Christ doth stand with the same mighty power of old. He is still the great Redeemer! I rest upon the promise that in His own good time He will say to the darkness which has come through sin, "Be dispelled!" and it shall be done. Strengthen me in this faith, for His name's sake. Amen.

❧ ❧ ❧

15. O Christ, I thank Thee for an inclusive gospel, that all men—the high and the low, the rich and the poor—can come into Thy presence with the same assurance of Thy compassionate love. The riches of Thy grace abound for all who commit themselves to Thee, for Thou art the Light of the world. May I confidently look forward to the day when all the world will find in Thee the fulfillment of its hope of salvation. In Thy name. Amen.

❧ ❧ ❧

16. Gracious Master, grant that I may never waver in my confidence that Thou art truly the Christ of God. Grant that I may forever hold fast my acceptance of Thee as my personal Redeemer. Keep aglow in my soul the joy of Thy salvation, and may I be forever Thine. In Thy name. Amen.

❧ ❧ ❧

17. Heavenly Father, I pray Thee that I may be with those whose sins have been forgiven, with those who believe on the Lord Jesus Christ, with those who are walking in His will, that I too may receive His benediction, "Fear not!" In His name. Amen.

❧ ❧ ❧

18. Merciful God, the giver of every good gift, I thank Thee for the assurance that the bondage of sin which holds so many in despair, in misery of soul, in helplessness, in

weakness, in shame, is completely broken when we turn to the Lord Jesus Christ with penitent hearts. Grant that we, afflicted by sin, may turn to Him with faith that He can, and will, save us from our sins and give freedom from any bondage. In His name. Amen.

ঌ ঌ ঌ

19. O Christ, I thank Thee for Thy gracious promise that if one has real faith, however small, any obstacle may be overcome. In accomplishing the tasks Thou dost assign or in bearing the burdens imposed by Thee, I thank Thee for the assurance that nothing is impossible to those who trust and obey Thee. Strengthen my faith, dear Lord, that I may not falter. In Thy name. Amen.

ঌ ঌ ঌ

20. Eternal God, help me to live in such vital touch with the blessed Christ that I may be endowed with the riches of His grace, so as to live daily the victorious life. May I be Spirit-filled and Spirit-led, each day bringing me to a fuller knowledge of Thee, a more complete dedication to the service of the Master, and a deeper assurance of salvation. In the name of Father, Son, and Holy Ghost. Amen.

ঌ ঌ ঌ

21. Almighty God, Thou hast created and redeemed my soul and body. Everything that I am or have is a gracious gift from Thee. May it please Thee to direct and hallow my thoughts, words, and deeds through this day, that I may use Thy gifts worthily. Hear my prayer. In His name. Amen.

ঌ ঌ ঌ

22. My Father, there is within me a passion for goodness. I desire it above all other things. I would stand before Thee redeemed from my sin and unrighteousness. Thou didst fashion me for this purpose, and I would appear before Thee

without spot or blemish. O give me of Thyself until my heart is satisfied. In the name of Christ my Lord. Amen.

❧ ❧ ❧

23. O Lord God, give me victory over the temptations of this day, and grant, I beseech Thee, that I may be diligent in Thy service. So order my life that it may conform to Thy holy will and be ever obedient to Thy commandments. Grant that my life may be hallowed by a deep sense of Thy presence, and, abiding in Thee, may be blessed with a sense of peace; through Jesus Christ. Amen.

❧ ❧ ❧

24. O Lord God, Thou who art the refuge of the distressed, the comforter of those in sorrow, I pray Thee to have compassion upon those whose hearts are heavily burdened in this world of tragedy. Grant deliverance, I beseech Thee, to all who are oppressed, and sustain those who are persecuted for righteousness' sake. Amen.

❧ ❧ ❧

25. O God, lead me out of the fog and mist of the valley and let me live upon the mountaintop with Thee. Grant that I may see all things from Thy point of view. Clarify my spiritual sight that I may see things at their real value. How worthless are so many of the things that the world clings to! Grant that I may daily lay up "treasures in heaven where neither moth nor rust doth corrupt, and where thieves do not break through nor steal." Amen.

❧ ❧ ❧

26. O God, may I listen to the wooings of Thy Holy Spirit with attentive ear. May Thy "still small voice" speak to my heart today and lead me into heavenly places. May my soul feast upon Thy truth as manna from heaven, for Jesus' sake. Amen.

27. O Lord Jesus, I thank Thee for the assurance of Thy friendship, that in Thee I have "a friend that sticketh closer than a brother." May I seek to be worthy of this relationship to Thee. For Thy name's sake. Amen.

❧ ❧ ❧

28. Dear Lord, teach me the secret of true discipleship. May no debasing influence come into my life. Open my mind and heart to Thy truth. Kindle anew in my soul a holy zeal for the things of the Spirit, for Thy sake. Amen.

❧ ❧ ❧

29. O God, I beseech Thee to strengthen my faith in Thy eternal goodness, that I may have a more wholesome outlook upon life in this confused world. Grant that I may have the faith that overcomes the world, a faith that can still trust when the clouds are the darkest, a faith that can know no defeat, a faith that will hold fast to Thee until the very end; through Jesus Christ my Saviour. Amen.

❧ ❧ ❧

30. Heavenly Father, I am thankful to Thee for the help found in Thee for the alleviation of all worry and care. Thou art infinite in power and changeless in Thy abounding love. Undergird my life with Thy presence, and give victory over all fear and doubt. May Thy children everywhere have the same security; through the Lord Jesus Christ. Amen.

❧ ❧ ❧

31. O Lord God of hosts, direct my mind by Thy gracious presence and give guidance to my daily walk with Thy fatherly love. Grant, I beseech Thee, that I may be enabled to live according to Thy holy will. Pardon my shortcomings. Give me greater zeal for Thee. Grant that I may be more diligent, under Thy leadership, in spreading a knowledge of Thy truth; through Christ my Lord. Amen.

1. O Jesus, Lover of my soul, Thou dost stand before Thy Father's throne making intercession for my soul. Thou art my Advocate, and my cause is in Thy hands. I am weak and full of sin, but Thou art full of grace and truth. The knowledge of Thy interceding in my behalf brings strength to my soul. I cannot fail today because Thou art holding me in Thy hands. In Thy name I pray. Amen.

ఎ ఎ ఎ

2. Almighty God, may the joy of Thy salvation flow into my heart as a river of refreshing water. May I find delight in keeping Thy commandments and in doing Thy will. May my soul be filled with "the peace of God, which passeth all understanding." In Christ's name. Amen.

ఎ ఎ ఎ

3. O Lord, I pray Thee to keep my heart warm today with the fire of the Holy Spirit. Overshadow my soul with Thy presence and give me a heart filled with love. May my soul have its delight in Thee and be attuned to the whisperings of the "still small voice." In Christ's name. Amen.

ఎ ఎ ఎ

4. O God, who art the Father of all men, give me a world-wide fellowship with Thy children of all races and classes. May I lift no exclusive barriers in my thinking or in my acts that spring from prejudice or a feeling of superiority and importance. I would embrace all men as brothers and strive to draw them within the company of the faithful of all ages. Grant that I may realize that all are one in Christ Jesus; for His name's sake. Amen.

ఎ ఎ ఎ

5. O God, give me grace to seek daily "those things which are above." Enable me to put off all wicked habits. Grant that all things of the flesh may be put to death and that I may know with ever greater and richer meaning what it

means to suffer with Christ. May I constantly assume nearer approaches to the perfection of Christ's image in my soul. In His name. Amen.

❧ ❧ ❧

6. O God, in Thee I put my trust. Thou art "the portion of mine inheritance and of my cup: thou maintainest my lot. . . . Therefore my heart is glad, and my glory rejoiceth: my flesh also shall rest in hope. . . . In thy presence is fulness of joy; at thy right hand there are pleasures forevermore." Unto Thee be the glory forever and ever. Amen.

❧ ❧ ❧

7. Heavenly Father, grant that my will may at all times harmonize with Thy will. As Jesus prayed in the darkest hour of His life, "Not my will, but thine, be done," grant that my will may be wholly yielded to the good and perfect will of God. May no sacrificial effort that may be required of me cause me to falter in Thy service in His name. Amen.

❧ ❧ ❧

8. O God, teach me the secret of inner peace. Strengthen my faith in Thee, so that I may not be haunted by fear. Give me the assurance that Thou art always near, and enable me to walk quietly and calmly. Give me that peace of mind and heart that the world cannot give or take away. unto Thee shall be the praise, through Christ. Amen.

❧ ❧ ❧

9. Heavenly Father, Thou art the source of all truth and wisdom. I pray Thee that I may be conscious always of Thy availability and of Thy never-failing love. I am grateful for the privilege of coming to Thee for quiet fellowship or in the hour of deepest need, knowing that Thou art sufficient for every need. In Christ's name I pray. Amen.

10. O Jesus, Thou Great Physician and Healer of men's souls, consider the weakness of my soul and impart Thy strength and power to me. Put Thy hand upon my sin wherever Thou dost see it and remove it from my life. Bind up my wounds and impart Thy calm to my spirit, and I shall yet praise Thee "who is the health of my countenance, and my God." Hear my prayer, for Thy name's sake. Amen.

⚜ ⚜ ⚜

11. Heavenly Father, deliver me from ill will, envy, jealousy, hatred, and all those things which hinder spiritual growth. Fill my heart with love for the beautiful and noble things of life and enable me to walk daily in the footsteps of Jesus. Help me to be worthy of all the good things with which Thou hast surrounded me. For Jesus' sake. Amen.

⚜ ⚜ ⚜

12. O God, teach me the secret of effectual prayer. When I pray for the coming of Thy Kingdom, lead me forth in the doing of Thy will. When I pray for deliverance from temptation, give me a will to shun the paths of temptation. When I pray for the redemption of men, make me an effective witness for Jesus Christ. In His name. Amen.

⚜ ⚜ ⚜

13. Spirit of God, breathe into my soul a hunger for righteousness, a spiritual unrest that will not cease until it has found satisfaction in Thee. Awaken in my heart a sense of need that will cause me to listen to Thy voice, as Thou makest known Thy love and care. Be very near to me in my daily walk; through Jesus Christ. Amen.

⚜ ⚜ ⚜

14. O my God, I thank Thee that Thou art my friend, and that there are holy intimacies between Thee and my

soul. I praise Thee that there is nothing which can destroy this blessed experience of fellowship with Thee. I thank Thee that I can find Thee in enduring reality through all expressions of Thyself in truth and beauty in this world and in traditional religion in its purest forms. Thou dost enter my heart through many avenues that I may never be unconscious of Thy presence. To Thee be all the praise, world without end. Amen.

❧ ❧ ❧

15. O Lord, Thou who art the Shepherd of my soul, lead me, I pray Thee, in paths of righteousness, that goodness and mercy may follow me all the days of my life. Thou art my God and I will praise Thee for ever and ever, through Jesus Christ my Lord. Amen.

❧ ❧ ❧

16. O Lord, God, Thou art my hope and refuge in time of trouble. In time of confusion, may I find the wave length that carries Thy voice. In time of danger, may I feel the undergirding of Thy presence. In time of anxiety, may I find comfort in Thy sustaining grace. Lead me through the darkness when it comes and strengthen me with the warmth of Thy unfailing love. Amen.

❧ ❧ ❧

17. Father in Heaven, I draw near unto Thee with confidence to seek Thy face, to understand Thy will and Thy purpose for me during this day. May I have the attitude of mind that was in Christ Jesus and be receptive always to Thy will. Override my mistakes of judgment and look with mercy upon those that are deliberate. Keep me from sin and strengthen me to do Thy holy will, through Jesus Christ my Lord. Amen.

18. My Father, grant that I may not measure the standards of my life by those of my fellow men. May I be satisfied with nothing less than the divine standard which Jesus revealed in His own character and in His dealings with men. May the glorious example of His life be ever before me. Relentlessly I would ascend the heights to which He summons His followers. No way is too steep, no road too rough if Thou art with me. Be Thou my guide through Jesus Christ my Lord. In His name I pray. Amen.

❧ ❧ ❧

19. O God, Thou hast given me the blessing of life. I would hold it as a stewardship from Thee. Forbid that I should yield to those temptations that would mar it. Save me from enmity against other men and from everything that is bad and mean in life. Forbid that I should be lured from the good life in Christ through any of the snares with which my daily walk is beset. In Christ's name. Amen.

❧ ❧ ❧

20. Heavenly Father, as I look back across the years, I have found that Thou art good. When dark clouds have come and fear would beset my path, faith in Thee and Thy fatherly care have lightened the way. Life, filled with memories of Thee at every turn, becomes richer as I journey through the years. In the blessed name of Christ, my Redeemer and Master. Amen.

❧ ❧ ❧

21. O God, I thank Thee for the desire to live and for that something which Thou hast placed in my soul that enables me to face the future in anticipation of a better day. Life is so saturated with Thy presence that it must have meaning and purpose. In the quest for life, my faith looks beyond the night to the dawn of a day in which there shall be no shadows. In Christ's name. Amen.

22. Infinite God, whose face is shown in the glories of Thy world, my soul is hushed as I look upon the beauties of Thy creation. Thus I come to meditate upon the things which Thou hast prepared for Thy children in a still fairer region beyond this life. In eternity this revelation shall be mine. Prepare me, O God, to receive this exceeding glory, and to know the beauty of holiness. In His name. Amen.

❧   ❧   ❧

23. Heavenly Father, the heavens and the earth are manifestations of Thy handiwork. All creation is aflame with Thy glory and is a revelation of Thy wisdom and Thy power. Grant, I pray Thee, that my heart may be responsive to all the beauty and splendor with which Thou hast adorned the world. Unto Thee I render the homage of my soul. Amen.

❧   ❧   ❧

24. Dear Lord, give me the power to look upon the world today with new eyes. Grant that old things pass away and all things become new. Let new hopes, new aspirations, new desires, spring within my soul; and new loves, new dedications, and new sacrifices control my life. I would be born again this day and be wholly Thine; for Jesus' sake. Amen.

❧   ❧   ❧

25. Heavenly Father, save me from a self-centered life. Give me a heart of pity and compassion as I face a needy and disturbed world. Defend me against any inclination toward bitterness, covetousness, or jealousy. May my heart be sensitive to the injustices of the world. Hear my prayer, which I offer in Christ's name. Amen.

❧   ❧   ❧

26. O Christ, I thank Thee that Thy Gospel is adequate for every need and that it sufficeth under the worst of life's

trials and burdens. "The Lord is my light and my salvation; whom shall I fear? The Lord is the strength of my life; of whom shall I be afraid?" Forbid that any sorrow should become so desperate or any cloud so dark as to close from view the light of heaven. In Thy name. Amen.

❧ ❧ ❧

27. Heavenly Father, I thank Thee for the Church and for the privilege of being among Thy people. Help me to be loyal to my vows of Church membership. How blessed it is to seek solace in Thy house when sorrow comes! When I am baffled with the ways of the world, what a privilege to find rest in Thy sanctuary. In Christ's name. Amen.

❧ ❧ ❧

28. Heavenly Father, give me a heart that is sensitive to the sufferings and needs of others. Give me the attitude of a soul which has lost its pride in the discovery of Thy mercy in its salvation. Give me a heart of compassion, kindness, lowliness, meekness, longsuffering; through Christ. Amen.

❧ ❧ ❧

29. Merciful God, save me from a life of complacency and easy-going. Deliver me from habits and practices which might hinder me in the attainment of Thy purposes for my life. Grant that I may not choose the easy way but the right way. Strengthen the fiber of my soul and endow me with a spirit of courage that will enable me to face victoriously any test. In Christ's name. Amen.

❧ ❧ ❧

30. O God, cleanse my heart of any unclean thing that may have found lodgment there. Fill my soul with holy desires, my mind with righteous thoughts, and my heart with noble purposes. May I abide in heavenly places with Thee and may my entire life abound in spiritual fruit. Amen.

1. Heavenly Father, I need spiritual anchorage, something to tie to which will hold me steady in these turbulent times. Grant that I may find such an anchorage through my Christian faith and experience. Thou art adequate for every need, and I know I cannot drift beyond Thy love and care. In Christ's name. Amen.

❧ ❧ ❧

2. Almighty God, from generation to generation Thou hast endowed man with wisdom and understanding of Thy purpose. Grant to me a portion of Thy Spirit that with humility I may serve Thee with understanding heart. May the need of this hour be a challenge to my mind, and the vision of a redeemed world be an inspiration to my soul. Breathe Thy Spirit upon me, and may all my days be bright with Thy presence; through Jesus Christ. Amen.

❧ ❧ ❧

3. Heavenly Father, I come into Thy presence with deep humility, mindful of my many shortcomings and of my unworthiness to stand in Thy holy presence. But Thou art the God of mercy and love, and it is with that assurance that I come before Thee to plead for forgiveness. Blot out my sins from the record books of life and lead me in the way of righteousness. In Christ's name. Amen.

❧ ❧ ❧

4. O God, give me guidance in disciplining myself that I may rise above the noise and tumult around me and find inward peace. Enable me to be more appreciative of the lovely things of life and of the kindly attitudes of my friends. When things are not as they should be, grant that I may be patient and able to fall back on reserves of spiritual strength that have been accumulated through quiet moments in communion with Christ. In His name. Amen.

5. Heavenly Father, this is Thy world in spite of all the strife and confusion prevailing among men. Make me aware of Thy presence; give me chart and compass that I may not become lost when clouds hang low. O God, sustain me by the power of Thy might and give me anchorage in Thy eternal verities; through Jesus Christ. Amen.

❧ ❧ ❧

6. O God, I humbly bow before Thee today and give Thee thanks for all the good along life's way. No matter what the days may bring, grief or joy, need or abundance, may I never, no never, lose sight of the eternal truth that this is my Father's world. In Christ's blessed name. Amen.

❧ ❧ ❧

7. O Thou great Shepherd of the souls of men, lead me through the valley of the shadows into green pastures. If I should stray away from Thy fold, bring me back again. When adversity comes, sustain me with Thy rod and Thy staff. May I find refreshment in the heat of the day in the overflowing cup of Thy blessings; through Jesus Christ our Lord. Amen.

❧ ❧ ❧

8. Gracious Lord, Thou hast said, "I am the way, the truth, and the life." Thou art ready to impart this life-giving power to me. Wilt Thou lead my soul today into the presence of God through the revelation of Thy truth, and grant unto me the power which alone can make me truly live. "As the hart panteth after the water brooks, so panteth my soul after Thee, O God." In Thy name I pray. Amen.

❧ ❧ ❧

9. O God, I worship Thee this day as my Maker, Redeemer, Friend. May I experience the fullness of Thy grace and care as I walk with Thee. How tender are Thy mercies!

How compassionate is Thy love! In Thee do I trust today, and in Thee will I trust to the end of life's journey; through my Lord Jesus Christ. Amen.

❧ ❧ ❧

10. Heavenly Father, I pray for a loosening of the bonds of material things upon my soul. May no earthly thing matter greatly to me. May the unseen and the spiritual be my greatest love, and the goal of my best effort. Touch my spirit and bind it with everlasting ties to Thyself. For the glory of Thy name I pray. Amen.

❧ ❧ ❧

11. O God, when the scope and outlook of my life become cramped and fettered, enable me to lift my horizons. When my work seems tedious, petty, or ineffective, enable me to understand that my chief work is to build a character fit for eternity. All else fades into insignificance, as compared with this holy task which Thou hast committed to me. May nothing mar this handiwork. In Christ's name. Amen.

❧ ❧ ❧

12. O God, I come to Thee for guidance because Thou hast said: "I will instruct thee and teach thee in the way which thou shalt go: I will guide thee with mine eye." Guide me aright, I pray Thee, and enable me to know, trust, and love Thee. Under Thy daily guidance may I experience more and more the warmth of Thy countenance and the blessedness of life with Thee. In Christ's name. Amen.

❧ ❧ ❧

13. O God, I come into Thy presence with a hungry heart. I pray Thee to lift me up above any mere argued beliefs about religion and enable me to grasp reality. Forbid that I should fail to obtain a vital experience of Thee through

any casual acceptance of an inherited faith. Give me an understanding of life's ultimate meaning that will hold me steady along life's way. In Christ's name. Amen.

❧ ❧ ❧

14. O God, grant that I may live in reverent fellowship with Thee and through that intimacy attain a knowledge of Thy purposes. Forbid that I should be so full of self, or so bent on attaining my own desires, that Thy will cannot be revealed to me. Give me the key to the Kingdom of Heaven, I beseech Thee, and enable me to walk in Thy ways by faith, through Jesus Christ. Amen.

❧ ❧ ❧

15. O God, grant that there may be in me a real and growing assimilation of Thy truth. Deliver me, I beseech Thee, from vain imaginations and unholy passions. Teach me to love and hate, to approve and condemn, in accord with the perfect model revealed in the Lord Jesus Christ. O give me this day Thy boundless grace. Amen.

❧ ❧ ❧

16. O God, I praise Thee for Thy abiding presence. It is as a sweet melody in my soul. I cannot escape its gracious thraldom. It interweaves itself in all my changing affairs. I sense it in my work and in my leisure. Thou art an abiding consciousness, and in Thee I move and have my being. For every manifestation of Thy presence, I give Thee praise; through our Lord Jesus Christ. Amen.

❧ ❧ ❧

17. O Christ, like the penitent disciple who had had much forgiven, I come before Thee and say: "Lord, thou knowest all things; thou knowest that I love thee." Thou hast toiled

and bled and died that my soul might be taken from the spoiler who has held it under his cruel and polluting sway. For Thy redeeming love, always so true and so abounding, I thank Thee, and, in turn, give Thee the fullness of my devotion. Amen.

❧ ❧ ❧

18. O God, teach me the secret of happiness, and enable me to express my love for Thee in nobility of character and unselfish conduct. There is no delight so deep and so true as the joy of doing Thy will. There is no blessedness like that of communing with Thee. Give me, I pray Thee, a clearer perception of Thy will, and harmonize my daily walk with Thy purposes. In Christ's blessed name I pray. Amen.

❧ ❧ ❧

19. O God, my soul seeks wistfully after Thee. Enable me to live very near Thee. Give me a spiritual insight that will dispel all doubts and misgivings. Enable me to heed the swift, inward impressions of Thy Holy Spirit. Unstop my ears, I pray Thee, and every sound borne through the silence will become a psalm of praise. In Christ's name. Amen.

❧ ❧ ❧

20. O God, give me an expectant and unwavering faith. Grant that I may say in the words of the psalmist, "My soul waiteth for the Lord more than they that watch for the morning." Undergird my supplications with an expectancy that Thy face shall shine upon me as certainly as the sun shall climb over tomorrow's horizon and dispel the shadows of night. Hear my prayer, O God, for Jesus' sake. Amen.

❧ ❧ ❧

21. Dear Lord, who once didst walk earth's rugged roads, wilt Thou look with compassion today upon my weakness

and weariness, for my strength is spent. I lift to Thee my empty up-turned cup and ask that Thou wilt fill it anew from Thy eternal reservoirs of strength and joy. Renew Thy Holy Spirit within me, O Lord, for Thy name's sake. Amen.

❧ ❧ ❧

22. O God, replenish my strength with the constant keeping power of Thy love. Enable me to meet daily with Thee in spirit until my life becomes lifted into blessedness and power. Grant that I may accept work as an opportunity to serve Thee today. So fill my life with a sense of fellowship with Thee that I may live and move and have my being in Thee; through Jesus Christ. Amen.

❧ ❧ ❧

23. O God, as I face the conflicts and perils and hardships of life, give me courage—that spark from Heaven's throne by which the soul stands triumphant. Enable me to be brave in the face of all opposition, scorn, and danger, when right is at stake. Anoint my soul with the presence of Thy Holy Spirit, give me the joy of Thy salvation, and enable me to perform every task committed to me with courage. In Christ's name. Amen.

❧ ❧ ❧

24. O God, enable me to realize that "in every sorrow of the heart, eternal mercy bears a part." Give me power to anticipate the morning in the night of grief and sorrow. Give me Thy companionship that I may have an unquenchable light burning within my heart, enabling me to see divine love in every pang and tear. I pray that the consolations of my faith in Thee will transform sorrow into joy and gloom into glory; through the Lord Jesus Christ. Amen.

25. O God, I pray Thee to lead me in the right way. Forbid that I should covet a life of ease and luxury. Thou knowest where and amid what experiences or conditions my life will best attain spiritual fruitage. Give me grace to endure any discipline that I may need to bring out the virtues of true Christian character. Enable me to look at life through divine purposes and find in it high and noble meaning, wherever my lot may be cast. In Christ's name. Amen.

❧ ❧ ❧

26. O Lord, as I come into Thy presence I would place my hand in Thine and commit myself wholly to Thy leadership. May my faith in Thee be so strong and my commitment to Thee be so complete that I may be ready and willing to follow wherever Thou dost lead. It may not always be amid joyous scenes, still it is enough to know that it is Thy hand that leadeth. Unto Thee I give the praise; through the Lord Jesus Christ. Amen.

❧ ❧ ❧

27. "Thy mercy, O Lord, is in the heavens; and thy faithfulness reacheth unto the clouds." The whole world abounds with manifestations of Thy loving-kindness and the provisions of Thy grace. In their midst I live and move and have my being. They come through a thousand channels and untold ways. Forbid, O Lord, that I should be an ungrateful steward of Thy treasures. In Christ's name. Amen.

❧ ❧ ❧

28. Heavenly Father, give me an understanding of Thy Word that I may find my way through the blinding illusions and delusions that beset me. May it be "a lamp unto my feet." "Open thou mine eyes, that I may behold wondrous things out of thy law." May Thy Word be as a compelling voice in my heart, awakening me to a new consciousness of my relation to Thee, my Maker. In Christ's name. Amen.

29. O God, when I am beset with cares, grant that my help may be found in Thee. Men in every age who have trusted in Thee have found contentment. Forbid, O Christ, that I should ever distrust Thee. Be Thou a sanctuary unto my soul. Give me freedom from fear and the frets of life. Keep me from evil. Give me an understanding of life in its relation to eternity, that I may be delivered from the dread of death; through Jesus Christ my Lord. Amen.

❧   ❧   ❧

30. O Lord, enable me to look to Heaven as the ultimate goal of all my hopes. May I live here with a view to life there with Thee. Guide me, I beseech Thee, in seeking those things in this life that will the better qualify me for that life. Enable me to work daily so that I may more and more possess a heavenly mind. In Christ's name I pray. Amen.

❧   ❧   ❧

31. O God, I thank Thee that I can come into Thy presence with a very simple trust in Thy keeping power. Surely Thou are mindful of the cries of Thy creatures. Thou dost guard Thy children from perils of the night and those of the day. May I rely upon Thee with an unfaltering trust, come what may. Sustain me, O God in all the changes and intercourses of my outward life as well as my most inward and secret life. May I abide with Thee now and forever; through the Lord Jesus Christ. Amen.

1. Holy Father, gird me by the power of Thy might, and make me to abide in security in the shadow of Thy presence. May Thy truth fill my mind and Thy love glow within my heart that I may be firmly bound to Thee. Awaken my spirit and clarify my vision that I may live nobly for Thee; through Jesus Christ my Lord. Amen.

※ ※ ※

2. Heavenly Father, I thank Thee for the privilege of prayer, for the opportunity to come to Thee with all my cares and anxieties and lay them before Thee. Grant that these moments alone with Thee may be a time of spiritual refreshment. Grant that I may gain strength in communion with Thee that will enable me to escape the tempter's snare and win the everlasting prize; through my Lord Jesus Christ. Amen.

※ ※ ※

3. Almighty God, as I face the trials and tribulations of life, I thank Thee for the power to live victoriously. With Thy servant of old, I can truly say, "I am persuaded that neither death, nor life, nor angels, nor principalities, nor powers, nor things present, nor things to come, nor height, nor depth, nor any other creature, shall be able to separate us from the love of God, which is in Christ Jesus our Lord." May this assurance hold me steady through the day. In Christ's name. Amen.

※ ※ ※

4. O God of infinite mercy, I am grateful for the revelation that Thou art a sin-forgiving God. In the depths of my weakness and sin, I can look unto Thee, as the God of my salvation. When I am disobedient and wayward, and out of the depths cry unto Thee, Thou art not afar off. Thou art full of forbearance. Then I lift my eyes again in adoration and in hope. Blessed art Thou, O God of love and mercy. In Christ's name. Amen.

5. O God, streams of bounty flow unceasingly from the fountains of Thy life. Thy infinite love so wondrously manifested deserves all my thought and meditation. And yet, how prone I am to become forgetful and unappreciative. It is so easy to take Thee and Thy gifts for granted. Forgive my thoughtlessness, and may every remembrance of Thee inflame my heart with a new sense of devotion to Thee. In Christ's name. Amen.

❧ ❧ ❧

6. O God, Thou who art long-suffering and most patient, I become perplexed when I go down into the secret depths of my soul. In those hidden depths, give me the light of understanding, O Lord, that I may see clearly what Thou dost will that I should do. Grant me divine grace, I beseech Thee, for the uprooting of all self-indulgence and self-will. May I never swerve in my obedience to Thee. In Christ's name. Amen.

❧ ❧ ❧

7. O Christ, who didst so love men that Thou didst choose to walk beside them in their way of weariness and toil, and who didst weep with them, give me a sympathy for men like unto Thine. I, too, would bear my brother's load and ease his daily burden. Give me a heart of tenderness toward all the lives I touch today. In Thy name. Amen.

❧ ❧ ❧

8. My Father, may deep, abiding love for all mankind transcend all other aims within my heart. May it free my heart from all concentration upon selfish desires and pleasures, and carry it out into joyous giving and sharing with others. Only so may my heart be drawn up into glorious fellowship with Thee, and only so may I share in bringing in Thy Kingdom on earth. In Christ's name, I pray. Amen.

9. Heavenly Father, I thank Thee that I am privileged to bring every burden of my soul to Thee—every hidden grief, every besetting sin, every sorrow—with the assurance that Thou art willing and ready to help one. Guide me by Thy Spirit, that I may avail myself day by day of Thy ever-present help, which Thou dost make available for all who trust in Thee. May I build the frail house of my life beneath the shadow of the Almighty, that in the day of sore need, I may surely find the way into the secret of Thy presence; through the Lord Jesus Christ. Amen.

❧ ❧ ❧

10. O God, there are times when Thou dost seem so far away, as completely out of my reach as if Thou madest Thy abode on some faraway planet. Forbid that I should lose my way, even though I may for the moment grope in the darkness. Even then may my song be: "A safe stronghold our God is still." In Christ's blessed name, I pray. Amen.

❧ ❧ ❧

11. O God, I would make Thee my refuge and my dwelling place. Enable me to live and dwell in Thee, to be nurtured by Thy loving care, to be fed by Thy bounty, and sustained by Thy mercy. In Thee may I find the answer to all my needs—protection against temptation, refuge from calamity, release from the burden of sin, consolation in the hour of sorrow. When my heart is tired and weary, may I find rest in Thee; through the Lord Jesus Christ. Amen.

❧ ❧ ❧

12. O God, I pray for wisdom to test my daily life in the light of its moral and spiritual issues. Give me the art of measurement, I beseech Thee, that will enable me to take precaution against the judgment to come, to make preparation for death, and the salvation of my soul. Forbid that I

should become so mindful of the things of this world that I should forget or neglect the real things of life that will prepare me for eternity. In Christ's name. Amen.

❧   ❧   ❧

13. Dear Lord, I pray that today I may be conscious of the needs of others, and look upon their afflictions with understanding eyes. Enable me to ease someone's burden in Thy blessed name. Accustom my soul to see Thee in the eyes of all needy men, and to minister to them as unto Thee. I would know the joy of giving the cup of cold water in Thy name. For Thine own sake, I pray. Amen.

❧   ❧   ❧

14. O God, enable me to enter into the innermost mysteries of life through the guidance of Thy Holy Spirit. Enable me, I beseech Thee, to dwell in the mystic abiding place of Thy presence, where celestial beings "rest not day and night, saying, Holy, holy, holy, Lord God Almighty." In nearness to Thee may life take on deeper meaning and sacredness. Give me, I pray Thee, a consciousness that Thou dost hear my prayer and accept the homage of my soul; through the Lord Jesus Christ. Amen.

❧   ❧   ❧

15. O God, teach me the secret of growth in character. Grant that I may acquire ruling convictions that are in harmony with Thy will. Give power to endure reverses when they come. Endue me, I beseech Thee, with refinement of feeling and all qualities of life that should mark a disciple of the Lord Jesus Christ. Amen.

❧   ❧   ❧

16. Gracious God, may I take the blessings Thou givest in germ and nurture them into full form. May I take the seed

Thou givest and wait patiently for them to grow into loveliness. Give me grace to accept the duties Thou dost place
before me, knowing that in their performance I shall discover
the secret of joy. May I toil for love's sweet sake and find in
every worthy act a rich sense of gladness, for Jesus' sake.
Amen.

❧ ❧ ❧

17. O God, give me grace to hold my desires in restraint
until Thou art ready to disclose Thy purposes. Forbid that
any ambition for place, recognition, or honor should mar my
growth in Christlikeness. May the chief desire be to repro-
duce, even though it be imperfectly, the loveliness of His
character. In His blessed name. Amen.

❧ ❧ ❧

18. O God, I thank Thee for the magnitude and mul-
tiplicity of Thy benefits. I am humbled in their presence
because they are unmerited. It is out of the graciousness
of Thy heart that I am made the recipient of Thy boundless
love. For every token of Thy love, I am truly grateful. Forbid that I should ever be an unworthy steward of Thy
benefactions. In Christ's name. Amen.

❧ ❧ ❧

19. O God, I will look up into Thy face, for there my
heart can rest, and all my fears are stilled. There I shall find
joy and peace and every hope fulfilled. I will surrender
myself to Thee, for Thou art my Lord, the desire of my heart.
Thou art all beauty and glory and strength, and at Thy
right hand there are pleasures forevermore. In holy exalta-
tion I bless Thy name and dedicate my all to Thee. In the
name of my blessed Lord. Amen.

❧ ❧ ❧

20. Heavenly Father, I am grateful unto Thee for the
privileges of the Christian Sabbath and all its holy associa-

tions. My Saviour has claimed it as His own and blessed it with the crowning fact of our holy religion, His resurrection from the dead. Forbid that any act of mine should ever desecrate that holy day or make it common in the sight of men. In Christ's blessed name. Amen.

❧ ❧ ❧

21. O God, I pray Thee for power to overcome those temptations that come to me when I am alone with my own thoughts. It is not alone for strength to vanquish the outward foe that I beseech Thee, but for deliverance from those besetting sins that steal into my thoughts with the stealth of some wild beast in the nighttime. Be Thou my helper and my deliverer, for Jesus' sake. Amen.

❧ ❧ ❧

22. Most gracious God, forbid that my sense of sin should become dim through familiarity, or that I should play with sin in any of its insidious forms, until the chains of habit become too strong for me to break. Deliver me from the temptation to substitute outward propriety for real character. May my inner life be such as to stand the test of Thy revealing light. In Christ's name. Amen.

❧ ❧ ❧

23. O God of divine grace, implant in my soul the seeds of holiness. Enable me in my daily walk to act in accordance with the principles of heavenly wisdom. Lead me by Thy almighty hand, and enable me to walk above the malign influences of this sinful world and follow the path that leads to eternal life; through the Lord Jesus Christ. Amen.

❧ ❧ ❧

24. O Christ, enable me to ascend the mount of holiness with Thee and dwell above the fogs of impurity and sin.

May I feast daily upon the Bread of Life in close and constant association with Thee. Endue me with Thy indwelling love, and enable me to keep the fountains of sympathy and brotherly kindness open and flowing day by day. In Thy blessed name, I pray. Amen.

❦ ❦ ❦

25. O Lord God, I stretch forth my hands to Thee. Turn not away from me, but receive me and embrace me in Thy everlasting love. It is through no merit of my own that I lay claim to Thy wondrous love but only through the merits of the cross and passion of the crucified Christ. In His name. Amen.

❦ ❦ ❦

26. O God, grant unto me that "fear of the Lord" which "is the beginning of wisdom." May Thy voice speak to my spirit and reveal unto me the true path for me to pursue in my daily walk. Enable me, I beseech Thee, to find peace and satisfaction for my life. Give me a deepened sense of Thy reality, for my soul yearns for something more than an intellectual grasp of Thee. It pants and thirsts for communion with Thee, the living God. Grant me this experience, I pray, in Christ's name. Amen.

❦ ❦ ❦

27. O Lord, when I lean upon my own understanding, I am weak and impotent. When I trust in Thee with my whole heart, I find strength for all my needs. May I never falter in my walk with Thee. May no passing clouds blur my vision of Thee. May a consciousness of Thy love today strengthen my faith in Thee for tomorrow. Hear my prayer, O God, for Jesus' sake. Amen.

28. Heavenly Father, I thank Thee for the assurance that Thou art active in all Thy creation, for the assurance that Thy presence fills the entire universe, and that Thou dost care for the welfare of all Thy creatures. There is nothing too vast or too trifling to escape Thy attention, for Thou art the God of all the universe. Wherever I am, or whatever I am doing, I would be conscious of Thy presence and of my reliance upon Thee. In Christ's name. Amen.

❧ ❧ ❧

29. O God, give me Thy guidance that I may lay hold on eternal life. May I possess the treasures of Thy Kingdom which are incorruptible. Enable me, gracious Lord, to lay up riches "where neither moth nor rust doth corrupt, and where thieves do not break through nor steal." Lift Thou the curtain of each new day, and may my delight be found in doing Thy will. Hear my prayer, for Jesus' sake. Amen.

❧ ❧ ❧

30. My Father, I thank Thee that Thou art a God of infinite love and mercy. One who dost mark even the sparrow's fall could not be otherwise. Help me to hold fast to this assurance, even when the mysteries of pain, the calamities of nature, the injustices of life may cloud my faith. Thou hast put Thy children into a stern school, but Thy love plans their glorious and ultimate redemption. I praise Thee, Father, for this faith. Amen.

❧ ❧ ❧

31. O Christ, what a price Thou hast paid for the redemption of my soul! When I remember Thy agony in the Garden, bent beneath the crushing burden of the world's sin, I begin to realize the cost of Thy mission of redemption. When I behold Thee in the darkness and solitude of the Cross, I can no longer trifle with sin. Grant that the very thought of it may be an abomination to my soul. In Thy blessed name. Amen.

1. O Lord, I thank Thee for this new day with its privileges and opportunities to serve Thee. Give me strength. Grant that Christ may permeate and ennoble everything I do. May there be nothing in the day's work that will make me ashamed when I stand in Thy holy presence on the day of final reckoning. In Christ's name, I pray. Amen.

❧ ❧ ❧

2. Heavenly Father, this is Thy world and I pray Thee to keep alive in my soul a deep sense of kinship with Thy children everywhere. Grant that no feeling of contempt may affect my attitude toward any of Thy children, regardless of race, color, or class. Help me to view all men as Thou dost view them. Enable me through my personal contacts to freshen their hope and joy in the faith. In His name. Amen.

❧ ❧ ❧

3. O Lord, how excellent are Thy works in all the earth! Keep before me the vision of the kind of world Thou wouldst have, a world in which righteousness, justice, peace, and good will prevail. Guide me in my daily walk that I may help make that kind of a world a reality. In His name. Amen.

❧ ❧ ❧

4. My blessed Lord, I praise Thee that Thou hast offered Thy friendship to me, and that I may enter into communion with Thee. Thou art by my side. Thou dost know me altogether, and before I call Thou dost answer me. This glorious thought makes every experience of life beautiful. Radiance falls upon life's path, for Thou art with me. Amen.

❧ ❧ ❧

5. O God, forbid that the flatteries of men should ever cause me to choose a way of life unworthy of a follower of Thee. Give me a discerning spirit and enable me to test the words of men in the crucible of Thy truth. Keep me strong in the inner man and may my spiritual vision be unmarred by unholy ambition. In Christ's name. Amen.

6. Heavenly Father, in Thy presence I am mindful of my imperfections. I have failed to realize so many of the noble purposes I have had in mind that I stand before Thee as if empty-handed. Forgive me wherein I have fallen short, and be Thou my teacher that I may become a master workman in Thy Kingdom, for Jesus' sake. Amen.

❧ ❧ ❧

7. O Lord, deliver me from those temptations that would lure me away from Thee. Grant that no desire to join the throng of those who feed upon the husks of pleasure or material wealth may ever dampen my ardor for the things of eternal worth. May I abide in peace in Thy highest contentment when greed or covetousness gnaw at my soul. In peace of heart may I serve Thee. In His name. Amen.

❧ ❧ ❧

8. Eternal God, give me an awareness of Thy presence everywhere I go. Clarify my sense of perception that I may see and understand the things of the Spirit. May everything I do this day be to Thy glory. As I tread the humble walks of life, grant that I may serve Thee. For His sake. Amen.

❧ ❧ ❧

9. Gracious Lord, who art from everlasting to everlasting, Thou dost wait patiently for the fulfillment of Thy plans. Give me of Thy patience. Help me to be patient with myself and with all other men. Grant that I may be long-suffering and calm amid annoyances. May the faults of others make me more watchful of my own shortcomings. I would be forgiving, for I, too, need Thy forgiveness. In Christ's name, I pray. Amen.

❧ ❧ ❧

10. O Lord, as I look out upon the heavens in their glory, my soul is thrilled with the beauty of Thy handi-

work. May the mystery of it all ever keep my soul attuned to Thee. I praise Thee for every thought of Thee that has lifted my soul, for every touch of Thy loving presence that has comforted me, for every relationship to Thee and to my fellows that has added to the beauty and sanctity of life. In Christ's name. Amen.

๕ ๕ ๕

11. O God, Thy redeeming love abides and endures when all else fails and passes away. Every day may I grow richer in the blessed life of the spirit. Enable me to walk in lofty altitudes with Thee. Increase my faith, deepen my humility, enlarge my spirit of reverence through companionship with Thee. In Christ's name. Amen.

๕ ๕ ๕

12. Heavenly Father, lift my horizons that I may see beyond the things that are into that future where destinies lie. Enable me to fit today's work into Thy eternal plan. Deliver me from every selfish purpose and enable me to serve Thee as a humble co-worker in the building of Thy Kingdom on earth. In Christ's name. Amen.

๕ ๕ ๕

13. O God, I thank Thee for the blessed hope of immortality. Quicken me by Thy mighty power that, dying unto sin, I may walk with Christ in newness of life. Grant that I may overcome all that is evil and displeasing to Thee. Give me the victory that overcomes the world, and bring me to everlasting life through Him who reigneth with Thee world without end. Amen.

๕ ๕ ๕

14. O God, in this hour of confusion and human need grant that I may live boldly with Christ, knowing that Thy Gospel is adequate for such a day as this. I would

look reality in the face with fearless eyes and be unafraid when I face the opposing forces of evil. May I live the Gospel today with a confident assurance of its ultimate triumph upon earth. In Christ's name. Amen.

※ ※ ※

15. O God of mercy and love, I throw open my heart and soul to Thee. In Thee I can take refuge from all my fears; in Thee I find the answer to my every need. When deep down in my heart there are feelings too sad or too sacred for utterance to mortal ears, when I crave for a deeper sympathy than that which man can give, my soul finds satisfaction in Thee. Forbid, O God, that I should seek other paths when I may walk with Thee. In His name. Amen.

※ ※ ※

16. O Spirit of God, baptize my soul with Thy holy presence and illuminate my vision with celestial light. Prepare me for high companionships, I pray Thee, and enable me to walk in the beauty of holiness. Bring into clearer light, I beseech Thee, Thy will and purposes that I may honor Thee with an understanding service. Amen.

※ ※ ※

17. O God, I have neither strength nor wisdom nor goodness of my own with which to meet some of the problems which face my life. I am helpless without Thee. But Thou art ever mindful of my need and hast bidden me to cast my care upon Thee. I lay these problems at Thy feet and ask that Thou wilt show me the way, O Lord, and I will walk in it. In Christ's name. Amen.

※ ※ ※

18. O God, forbid that I should ever shun the "Way of the Cross," even though it be a difficult and rugged way. Give me grace to adhere to the principles of Christ, even

though it may mean trouble, discomfort, and sacrifice. O give me, I pray Thee, grace to endure in the face of all criticism or personal loss. In Christ's name I pray. Amen.

*   *   *

19. O God, my Father, for every seemingly unanswered prayer help me to see the better gift which comes from Thy hand. Thou dost always hear me when I come to Thee and Thou dost give what in Thy infinite wisdom Thou seest is best for me. May I never doubt Thy wisdom or Thy love, when the things for which I ask are denied, for Thou dost answer all my prayers. Teach me to love Thy will. Amen.

*   *   *

20. O God, may Thy presence abide with me in my daily work. May the light of Thy countenance brighten and make clear my earthly path. Abide Thou with me as a continual source of spiritual strength and nourishment. Give me understanding that I may walk according to Thy blessed will; through the Lord Jesus Christ. Amen.

*   *   *

21. Gracious Lord, take from my heart all fear, for it is like a crouching beast that would tear away all peace from my heart. I would place my hand in Thine and know the power that is sufficient for all things that may ever come into my life. Thou art the source of all hope and joy, therefore will I put my trust in Thee. In Thy blessed name. Amen.

*   *   *

22. Eternal God, I thank Thee for the boundless fullness of Thy love. What treasure of mercy is possessed by those who can say, "O God, Thou art my God"! I believe in Thee, I reverence Thee, I worship Thee, O Lord God. For Thy redeeming love in Christ Jesus I shall praise Thee until my dying breath. In His blessed name. Amen.

23. O Thou who art the delight of my soul and the joy of my life, I thank Thee that I am Thy child. My thirsty heart finds refreshment in Thee and strength for all my needs. Thou dost fill my heart with continual praise. My spirit leaps and sings when I think upon Thee. Thy love overflows my heart. Thy mercy is boundless. I will praise Thee forever and ever. Amen.

❦ ❦ ❦

24. O God, today I dedicate all that I am, all that I have, all my desires to Thee. With a sure and steadfast faith, with a simple but unwavering trust, I commit myself to Thy keeping. I would lose my life completely in Thee. Use it in holy tasks for Thy glory; through Christ. Amen.

❦ ❦ ❦

25. O God, forbid that I should let slip today any of the opportunities that may confront me for laying up treasure in heaven and for promoting Thy glory. Deliver me from all false doctrine, and enable me, I beseech Thee, to stand forth in the faith. Enable me to keep my heart with all diligence and deliver me from any spirit of worldly-mindedness. Give me victory over all spiritual enemies that encompass me; through the Lord Jesus Christ. Amen.

❦ ❦ ❦

26. Heavenly Father, let all the earth render praise unto Thee, for Thou alone art God and worthy of the worship of men. Bring in Thy Kingdom on earth, so that peace and righteousness may prevail throughout all the earth. Enable me to live in such intimate fellowship with Thee day by day that I may effectively witness for Thee in the advancement of Thy Kingdom. In Christ's name. Amen.

27. Eternal God, Thou art long-suffering and most patient to have borne with me as Thou hast. Sustain me, I pray Thee, when life seems intolerable, and enable me to walk by faith with Thee. When temptations would drag me down, give me courage to overcome. For Jesus' sake. Amen.

ж ж ж

28. Almighty God, be Thou a lantern for my path and a light for my feet. It is in Thy light that I am able to perceive the deeper meaning of life. It is only in communion with Thee that my eyes are illumined, and I am enabled to see the glories and realities of the spiritual universe. Forbid that I should walk alone in shadowed valleys, or grope in perplexity when I am privileged to walk with Thee in the light. Hear my prayer, for Jesus' sake. Amen.

ж ж ж

29. O God, give me a sure consciousness of Thyself. Open my eyes that I may see Thee. When I apply myself to my daily work, give me the grace to continue in Thy presence. If I have Thee as an enduring presence, I am no longer at the mercy of life's fluctuations. In plenty or in need, my meat and drink is to do Thy will, through the Lord Jesus Christ. Amen.

ж ж ж

30. O God, Thou who dost mold all life to Thine own purpose, freshen my appreciation of Thy wondrous ways of achievement. May I never view lightly even the smallest events and circumstances, for they may be of Thy making. Teach me the value of being mindful of the seemingly insignificant things, for they are so often the decisive. Joy or sorrow may follow in the wake of the trifles of my daily life, dependent upon their regulation by Thy holy will. In Christ's name. Amen.

1. My Father, in this new dawn I give Thee thanks for the rest of the night that is past, and for the joy of a new day. Draw me to Thyself that I may live in Thee. Banish the mistakes of yesterday, old worries, old fears. Grant that with an eager heart I may take up the tasks of the day. May I labor with a single purpose—to do Thy perfect will and to glorify Thy holy name. In the name of Jesus Christ my Lord, I pray. Amen.

❧ ❧ ❧

2. O God, who art eternal Love, I lift my heart to Thee and ask that I may perfectly follow Thee today in a straight path and with a single purpose. Instil within my soul Thy nature, and encourage all heavenly virtues within me. Witness within my heart that I am Thy child; for the sake of Jesus Christ my Saviour. Amen.

❧ ❧ ❧

3. O God, who art the Father of all mankind everywhere, teach me the full significance of my relationship to Thee and to my fellows. May no man, of whatever race or language, who bears the divine impress, be regarded as common. School and discipline the nations of men until they shall become conscious of Thy fatherhood and dwell together in the unity of brotherhood; through the Lord Jesus Christ. Amen.

❧ ❧ ❧

4. Heavenly Father, I recognize Thy divine authority and pray that Thou wilt give me right motives. Forbid that I should be guilty of the hypocrisy of doing good merely to be seen of men. Grant that all things may be done with a very real desire to be well pleasing to Thee. Hear my prayer, which I offer in the name of Thy dear Son. Amen.

5. O my Father, wilt Thou give unto me a divine sense of mission in life. May I be able to say with Thy Son, "To this end was I born, and for this cause came I into the world." May I press forward toward the goal for which I have been apprehended by Jesus Christ. Place upon my life the touch of Thy hand and give me the consciousness that I am being used of Thee in some worth-while task. In the name of my blessed Lord. Amen.

❧ ❧ ❧

6. O Thou divine Teacher, enrich my mind with a grasp of new truths as I sit daily at Thy feet, and give me a deeper understanding of the laws by which the world is governed. Enable me to discern more intelligently, I beseech Thee, the marvels of beauty and design in Thy universe, and to grasp with clear understanding the conditions of human progress. In Thy name. Amen.

❧ ❧ ❧

7. Heavenly Father, Thou who hast given me life, enable me to glorify Thee through worthy service. Thou hast first place in my life. Forbid, I pray Thee, that any personal ambition or unworthy purpose should tempt me to become unmindful of the stewardship Thou hast committed to my hands. Forbid that I should sit idly by, merely as an onlooker, when there is so much to be done. In Christ's name. Amen.

❧ ❧ ❧

8. Gracious God, grant that my life may have deep roots in Thy eternal life. As the storms beat upon the tree of my life, may its roots take deeper hold, and its boughs drink new beauty from the wind and rain, which tosses and bends them low. Defeat and failure, sorrow and despair can serve to make me strong. Grant today that I may drink of Thy

infinite power. Bring Thou triumph out of my struggle and pain. In the name of Jesus Christ my Redeemer. Amen.

※ ※ ※

9. O God, teach me the virtue of self-control, and grant that all my appetites, thoughts, and imaginations may be held in captivity for Christ. May my inner life be regulated at all times by a purpose and will to keep it pure and worthy of Thee. Teach me the discipline of self-denial, that I may be strong to resist indulgence in things unlawful in Thy sight; through the Lord Jesus Christ. Amen.

※ ※ ※

10. Merciful God, may I find joy in obedience to Thy laws. Thou dost govern the world through laws that are just, good, and holy. In the keeping of them there is great reward. But Thou art more than an exacting Lawgiver; Thou art a gracious Father, offering salvation to all men through faith in the Lord Jesus Christ. May I honor Thee in the keeping of Thy commandments and enjoy security and liberty in Thy abounding grace. In Christ's name. Amen.

※ ※ ※

11. My Saviour, let me walk alone today in the green pastures of Thy love. Amid the distractions and cares of the day I would be conscious of Thy indwelling presence which is the source of my strength and joy. Let me know the peace which passeth understanding, as I lean my head upon Thy breast; for Thy dear name's sake. Amen.

※ ※ ※

12. Heavenly Father, may I spend much time alone with Thee and in that communion find strength and spiritual power. Deliver me from unreality or pretended earnestness. In solitude with Thee, may I find reality in my spiritual experience. Cheer my soul with a sense of Thy presence and

enable me to press forward with unfaltering step in Thy service. In Christ's name. Amen.

❧ ❧ ❧

13. O God, enable me to fill worthily that place in life to which Thou hast called me. Forbid that this desire should become disfigured or degraded by any selfish ambition. Fill my soul with a holy vision of a world patterned after Thy will, and enable me to do my part in making that vision a reality, for Jesus' sake. Amen.

❧ ❧ ❧

14. O God of mercy and love, I throw open my heart and soul to Thee. From Thee nothing is hidden. Search me, purify me, lead me in the way everlasting. Thou hast said, "If a man love me, he will keep my words: and my Father will love him, and we will come unto him, and make our abode with him." Thou art the one in whom I can take refuge in all my needs. When deep down in my heart there are feelings too sad and too sacred for utterance to mortal ears, when I crave a sympathy higher than that which man can give, my soul finds relief and satisfaction in Thee. For all these things I give Thee humble and grateful thanks; through Jesus Christ our Lord. Amen.

❧ ❧ ❧

15. O God of all grace and comfort, when I would grow sad with longing for those whose faces I no longer see and whose voices are forever still, help me to remember that they and I are members still of Thy family whether in heaven or on earth. Prepare me for the unspeakable joys of the life to come when we shall rejoice in the fullness of Thy love forever; through Jesus Christ our Lord. Amen.

❧ ❧ ❧

16. O God, I thank Thee for the redeeming and sanctifying power of Christ in my life. It is, indeed, the power of

God unto salvation—a salvation from the bondage of sin, a salvation which imparts a consciousness of eternal life. The tender breathings of Thy love envelop my soul and enable me to yearn for Thee wherever I am. Oh, may Thy presence be constant and abiding. In Christ's name. Amen.

❧ ❧ ❧

17. Holy Father, implant within me a passion for sacrificial living, for only such a life can have an intimacy with Jesus. Awaken my soul from selfish ease and indolent living that Christ may minister to men through my daily life. Help me to recognize my own responsibility for the sufferings of the poor and needy. Give me the heart of a brother toward my fellow men. May I be strong and wise and tender in their behalf. For Jesus' sake. Amen.

❧ ❧ ❧

18. O God, endue me with power to conquer the fear, the selfishness, the covetousness, the unworthy ambitions, the pettiness of spirit, which have spoiled so many of my days. Make me a help rather than a hindrance, I beseech Thee, to those whose lives are bound up in any way with mine. Awaken through Thy Holy Spirit any latent powers within me and enable me to live at my best. In Christ's name and for His sake. Amen.

❧ ❧ ❧

19. My blessed Lord, I pray for an attitude of cheerfulness and love toward my work. May all self-seeking and self-will be put aside, and may the glory of God be my only desire. May I be as faithful in the little duties of the day as in the greater ones, for Thou, O Lord, alone canst be the judge of their importance. May my work today bear the mark of faithful stewardship. In Christ's name. Amen.

20. Lord Jesus, be Thou my hope and stay. Deliver me, I pray Thee, from the presence and dominion of sin. Give me the victory of faith and hope, and make me right with the whole order of the things of God. Enable me to shake off any lethargy which may numb my soul. In Thy blessed name I pray. Amen.

❦ ❦ ❦

21. O God, I thank Thee for Thy revelation concerning the judgment to come. Forbid that I should ever become indifferent to Thy warnings and importunings. Forbid that either the cares or the enjoyments of this world should cause me to lose sight of any accountability to Thee. Deliver me from the temptation to procrastinate or compromise with evil in any form. Hear my prayer, for Jesus' sake. Amen.

❦ ❦ ❦

22. O God, may Thy Spirit move mightily in the heart of the Church, quickening its spiritual life with renewed power. Descend upon it, O Spirit of God, with purifying fire till it is purged of all that is base, false, and earthly. May it reflect the beauty and loveliness of the eternal glory of Thy Son. Make it a holy Church and an effectual witness in these days of desperate need. In Christ's name I pray. Amen.

❦ ❦ ❦

23. O God, enable me to live daily in the spirit of harmony with Thy will. Endue me with aspirations to live in Thy service only, for life begins and ends in Thee. Without Thee, life holds no worthy purpose. May my mind rise above all petty aims and selfish interests, and may my desires find their fulfillment in doing Thy holy will; through the Lord Jesus Christ. Amen.

❦ ❦ ❦

24. "Come, Thou Fount of every blessing,
     Tune my heart to sing Thy grace."

Thou art the fountainhead of all my joy and I would praise Thee through days of sunny traveling and through days of weary marching. I thank Thee for the joy of knowing Thee, and loving Thee, for the joy of doing Thy will. In Thy presence there is fullness of joy. In the name of Jesus Christ. Amen.

※ ※ ※

25. O God, Thou art the home of my soul, and apart from Thee I have no fixed abode. To live and dwell in Thee, nurtured by Thy loving care, fed by Thy infinite bounty, sustained by Thy infinite grace, what else shall I want? My sufficiency is in Thee. With Thee as my habitation, all my wants are supplied. Unto Thee be all praise, world without end. In Christ's name. Amen.

※ ※ ※

26. O God, I thank Thee for the revelation through Christ of Thy interest and concern for all men. But too often we have been so reluctant to do Thy will. We have permitted our own selfishness and greed to thwart the coming of Thy Kingdom. It is not Thy will that the world should plunge itself into conflict and anguish and death. Let Thy Spirit move upon the face of the earth, bringing men to penitence; through the Lord Jesus Christ. Amen.

※ ※ ※

27. Gracious God, grant that I may learn to give myself more earnestly to the practice of prayer. May my spirit long for communion with Thee as my physical body craves food and drink. Teach me how to wait patiently before Thee and kindle within me the flame of expectancy. There is something Thou wouldst say to me alone each day. Thou art yearning to impart a message to my soul. O give me a listening ear. In Jesus' name. Amen.

28. O God, so fill my heart with the grace of Thy love that I may be unmindful of the slights of men. When any wrong or injury rankles in my soul, heal its wounds and save me from the virus of revenge. Forbid that any passing irritation by some thoughtless one should rob my soul of its joy in Thee. In Christ's name. Amen.

❧ ❧ ❧

29. Heavenly Father, may I be conscious of my infinite worth in Thy sight. May I realize in part what it means to be a son of God, and may my conduct be becoming to this high estate. May I never grieve Thy Holy Spirit by low living or unworthy actions. Endue me with power that I may grow in the image of Thy Son, my Saviour. In the name of Jesus Christ. Amen.

❧ ❧ ❧

30. Heavenly Father, grant that the things of God may have priority always in my life. May the petty and trivial be crowded out by a mastering sense of spiritual values. Give my life the lift that comes through the consciousness of Thy presence, and I will give Thee the praise; through Jesus Christ my Lord. Amen.

❧ ❧ ❧

31. O God my Father, Thou dost know me altogether. Thou canst see the depths of my heart. Thou alone knowest the deep longings, the secret sins, the keen temptations, the hidden griefs, the bitter disappointments of my soul. Shine into the depths of my being and illumine me by Thy heavenly presence.

> "No human heart can enter
> Each dim recess of mine
> And soothe and hush and calm it
> O blessed Lord, like Thine."

In His name. Amen.

1. O Christ, to whom hast been given all authority in heaven and on earth, I bow humbly in Thy presence and submit my will to Thine. While here in the flesh Thou didst teach in a manner that won the admiration of Thine adversaries. Thou didst exercise Thine authority in healing all manner of disease, in cleansing the leper, in casting out demons, and in raising the dead. I praise Thy blessed name and am thankful that I can call Thee my Saviour. Amen.

※ ※ ※

2. O Christ, I pray that my manner of life may be a worthy testimony for Thee. As an "epistle" of Thine, grant that the writing may not be blurred or blotted, but that it may be such as may be known and read of all men. Grant that I may not be baffled with doubts, but that I may be sustained by a faith that attests Thy reality. Hear my prayer, for Thy name's sake. Amen.

※ ※ ※

3. O Lord, take my hand and guide me over life's devious paths. Uphold me in times of weakness or uncertainty. Manifest Thy affection and tenderness when my heart is faint and failing. Cheer my soul at all times with a sense of Thy presence. Hear my prayer, O Lord, for Thy blessed name's sake. Amen.

※ ※ ※

4. O Christ, I would share Thy cross with Thee. Dark indeed is the path of the cross, yet that is where I may come to know Thee best. It is here that Thou didst find Thy greatest glory. Walk with me in the dark and bitter experiences of life, and out of them may I behold in greater clarity Thy glory. In Thy name. Amen.

※ ※ ※

5. O God, I venture my all upon Thee. With a sure and steadfast faith, with an unswerving trust, I give myself,

my all, into Thy keeping. Open the doors of heaven, I pray Thee, and may new vistas of faith be opened to my soul. Enrich my inner life through an ever-enlarging spiritual insight, through the Lord Jesus Christ. Amen.

※ ※ ※

6. O Holy Spirit, enlighten my conscience and control my will to the end that I may be led to an acknowledgment of my sin, to repentance, and to belief in my Saviour. Forbid that I should grieve Thee, O Spirit of God, by rejecting Thy testimony or by refusal to heed Thy importunings. Keep me ever sensitive to Thy wooings; through the Lord Jesus Christ. Amen.

※ ※ ※

7. O God, as I come into Thy presence, I lay my hand in Thine, ready to do Thy will. May I have a sense of Thy nearness in my daily walk. May I bring some sunny brightness, some cheery confidence, some holy peace into the circle in which I move today, because I have been with Thee. Be Thou as a fountain of living water in my soul; for Jesus' sake. Amen.

※ ※ ※

8. My Lord, I pray that today Thy will may be done in the lives of those dearest to me. Give them a desire to please Thee, strengthen them to endure, comfort them by Thy grace, lead them in wisdom's ways, and show them Thy face. Lead them in paths of righteousness for Thy name's sake. Amen.

※ ※ ※

9. Heavenly Father, deliver me from the sin of empty profession. Give me a vital faith, a faith based upon a deep sense of the reality of spiritual things. Grant that I may never waver in my loyalty to Thee. Purge my heart of envy, greed,

pride, intolerance, bigotry, and all things that thwart my spiritual growth. In Christ's name. Amen.

❧ ❧ ❧

10. Heavenly Father, grant that the enjoyment of the comforts of life may be to me a daily reminder of my responsibility to those less privileged. As I partake of my food, may I be mindful of my duty to minister to Thy children who are without food or shelter. Grant that the enjoyment of the fellowship of friends and home may be a reminder of those who are denied this privilege. May I seek to share that fellowship with them. For Jesus' sake. Amen.

❧ ❧ ❧

11. Heavenly Father, this is Thy world, though it may be a prodigal world. It is passing through the refiner's fire. Grant that the consciousness of redemptive love, as manifested on the Cross, may permeate the life of world. Grant that an awareness of that love may constrain men increasingly to seek to live together in peace and mutual helpfulness; through the Prince of Peace. Amen.

❧ ❧ ❧

12. O God, deliver Thy Church from that miserable contentment with things as they are, that attitude of mind which is so prevalent. Deliver Thy people from desires that are narrow, selfish, and small. Create in Thy Church, O God, that hunger and thirst for righteousness which belong to the blessed. In Christ's name. Amen.

❧ ❧ ❧

13. Dear Master, I would not ask to follow the easy way of life, for that was not the way Thou didst walk. Reveal unto me my duty as a disciple of Thine and give me guidance that I may be faithful in its performance. Enable me to

forget self in Thy service. I offer this prayer in Thy name, my Lord and Redeemer. Amen.

❧ ❧ ❧

14. O God, may I this day dwell in the secret place of the most High and abide under the shadow of Thy wing. Here I would seek refuge when the storms arise or temptations beset me. Thou art a very real shelter for my soul. Hear my prayer, which I offer in the name of Thy Son Jesus Christ. Amen.

❧ ❧ ❧

15. O Lord God Almighty, I bow in Thy presence, conscious of my own frailties and need of Thee. Thou art so full of understanding and vision; Thou art so merciful and loving that I come to Thee with the assurance that Thou art the answer to the deeper needs of my soul. Break Thou unto me the bread of life and minister unto my needs out of the fullness of Thy understanding. In Christ's name. Amen.

❧ ❧ ❧

16. My Father, in hours of pain Thou art strangely near. Thou dost teach us life's deepest lessons and sublimest truths through the bitter experiences of life. May I never shrink from sorrow, disappointment, or loss, but face them calmly, bravely, even joyfully, knowing that through them life's deepest enrichments come. I yield my pain to Thee, O God, that it may become my servant and not my master. In the name of Him whose suffering sealed my redemption and life forevermore. Amen.

❧ ❧ ❧

17. Heavenly Father, I pray Thee for an assurance that I am a child of Thine. May I be led into such intimate communion and fellowship with Thee that I may have the joy of knowing that my sins have been forgiven. Bear Thy

witness to my soul, O God, and I shall praise Thee before men. Day and night I hunger and thirst for Thee, and apart from Thee I find no abiding peace and satisfaction. Amen.

⁂

18. God of all wisdom and truth, teach me, I pray Thee, to flee from temptation and to shun unruly appetites. Endue me with the spirit of tolerance that I may not pass harsh judgments on others. Teach me to be more unselfish, more kindly, more helpful in all my contacts with my fellow men. In Christ's name. Amen.

⁂

19. Holy Father, forbid that I should ever be indifferent to the sorrow and suffering of others. May Thy presence in my own life be so manifest that I may carry a healing balm to those in need. Look with compassion, I pray Thee, upon the ills of men everywhere, for Jesus' sake. Amen.

⁂

20. O God, most gracious Father, deal with me in all of life's situations as Thou thinkest best. Thy will, not mine, be done. My life is committed unto Thee. I will follow wherever Thou dost lead, whether it be in health or affliction. It is enough to know that Thou art with me. In Christ's name. Amen.

⁂

21. O God, deliver me from neutrality in a world where issues are clearly drawn between good and evil. Forbid that I should do as others when I am in an environment where Thy name is not revered. So order my manner of life that all men may know that my lot has been cast with Thee. Hear my prayer, for Jesus' sake. Amen.

⁂

22. O God, sustain me when I am puzzled and perplexed and unable to understand why Thy children suffer

so many disappointments in their daily walk. Grant, O merciful God, that I may walk by faith when Thy purposes are not made clear or when Thou dost withhold the answer to my prayers. Permit nothing to blight for even a moment my confidence in Thy goodness and love. In Christ's name. Amen.

$$\ast \quad \ast \quad \ast$$

23. O God, I pray Thee to guide me in the doing of Thy will and in the achievement of Thy purpose for me. Strengthen and fortify my soul against temptation. Teach me the ways of holiness, and grant that I may stand before Thee with a clear mind and a clean heart. Unto Thee would I commit my all, for Thou art my Maker and my Redeemer. In Christ's name. Amen.

$$\ast \quad \ast \quad \ast$$

24. Heavenly Father, I am grateful for Thy Spirit of compassion as revealed in the life of Thy Son Jesus Christ. When I face all the need and suffering in the world, I know that Thou art not unmindful of these things. I praise Thy name that it is no vain hope that the time will come when all life's needs will be abundantly met, for I have Thy promise that it will be so. In Christ's name. Amen.

$$\ast \quad \ast \quad \ast$$

25. O Lord God, I come into Thy presence with a deep appreciation of Thy holiness and goodness. All Thy works on earth, in the sky, and on the sea reveal Thy kindly providence and enable me to cast myself down before Thee in holy adoration. My life shall ever praise Thee, for there is no other so perfect in power and purity. May I be worthy to call Thee Father, through Jesus Christ my Lord. Amen.

$$\ast \quad \ast \quad \ast$$

26. O God, I thank Thee for the holy memories which overflow my heart, memories of my parents' love, and my childhood joys, my early hopes and aspirations which came

from Thee. I thank Thee for the fuller fruition of the years, the ripening friendships, the blessings of my home and children, the joy of tasks accomplished in Thy name and for Thy sake. But above all these, dear Lord, I thank Thee that Thou hast given Thyself to me. Amen.

❧ ❧ ❧

27. O God, forgive me when I become impatient at Thy seeming leisure with the world. Give me a patient heart while Thou dost wait to work out Thy vast plan. Hush every fret and murmur and disturbing thought. Give me the strength to suffer, the willingness to sacrifice, the power to endure under protracted or aggravated trials for Thy sake. Give me these inward ministries of strength and consolation, for Jesus' sake. Amen.

❧ ❧ ❧

28. Heavenly Father, help me to make right choices day by day. Life is so complicated that I need Thy guidance at every turn of the road. Lead me, I beseech Thee, into a finer sympathy with the things that are good and sacred in Thy sight. In Christ's name. Amen.

❧ ❧ ❧

29. O Lord, I pray for Thy Church that it may be kept pure and unspotted from the world. Give guidance to those who minister at its altars, and may it ever bear true witness for Thee. Within its sacred walls may I find consolation in time of deepest need. In it, may I enjoy communion with Thee and sweet fellowship with others who are brethren. In Christ's name. Amen.

❧ ❧ ❧

30. O merciful and gracious God, renew my faith in Thee, my hope for the future, and my love for Thy Kingdom. Renew my mind and heart that I may be more fully consecrated to Thee, and that I may serve Thee more diligently. Renew my desire to walk in the light of Thy truth and in the strength of Thy Spirit; through Jesus Christ the Lord. Amen.

1. O Lord, I come before Thee at the beginning of this day as a pupil to his teacher. I love to sit at Thy feet and learn of Thee, for in Thee do I find the way of life. Indeed, Thou hast said, "I am the way, the truth, and the life." Teach me today to do the things that are pleasing to Thee and keep me in the way everlasting. In the name of Jesus Christ my Lord and Saviour. Amen.

*   *   *

2. O Lord, I crave the peace and satisfaction that can come through an intimate relationship with Thee. Give me this day the full consciousness that my life is attuned to the divine forces that are operative in the world of Thine. Grant that I may be so led by Thy eternal Spirit that my life may never run counter to Thy plans and purposes, but may blend in with them and move forward in unison with them. For Thy name's sake. Amen.

*   *   *

3. O my Father, save me from an attitude of fault-finding and of criticism of others in my daily life. Grant that I may see the good in all men and magnify their virtues, remembering that Thou dost deal thus graciously with my own imperfections. May I see in others what I long for Thee to see in my own life, a likeness to Thee. Give me a gentle consideration for human weakness in all men; for Christ's sake. Amen.

*   *   *

4. O Lord, I shall come in contact today with sorrow, suffering, and sin. In those contacts may I carry a helpful and victorious spirit. May it be the spirit of one who knows the saving power of Jesus Christ and the joy of having Him as a daily companion. In His name. Amen.

*   *   *

5. Almighty God, save me from spiritual delusions and enable me to live life at its best. Empower me that I may

"hold fast the confidence and the rejoicing of the hope firm unto the end." May I seek first the Kingdom of God and at all times heed the upward call of Jesus Christ. May my soul be so deeply anchored in Him that I may be able to withstand any storm. In His name. Amen.

❧ ❧ ❧

6. O God, be merciful unto me and bless me. Remember not my iniquity, but spare me whom Thou hast redeemed with the precious blood of Thy Son Jesus Christ our Lord. Be Thou my strong defense and deliver me from the snares of the evil one. May I go forth today in the strength of the Lord. Amen.

❧ ❧ ❧

7. O Lord God, intensify my hunger for the things of the Spirit and give me the joy of the life abundant. Create in me a clean heart, and may I have divine guidance in order that my daily walk may be worthy of one who professes faith in the Lord Jesus Christ. Amen.

❧ ❧ ❧

8. Heavenly Father, wilt Thou touch my lips today with gentleness and kindness that my speech may bring cheer and comfort to my fellow men. May no careless, unkind, or untruthful word mar the beauty of the day for any heart. Speak through my lips and draw men unto Thee by the winsome beauty of Thy love. For Thy name's glory. Amen.

❧ ❧ ❧

9. Heavenly Father, I thank Thee for the gift of this new day. Forbid that I should become so absorbed in petty things that I may be unmindful of Thee and those spiritual values which enrich life and give it real meaning. Open the eyes of my spiritual understanding that I may discover Thy will in all things; through Jesus Christ the Lord. Amen.

10. O Christ of God, my life is so often filled with unrest because of lack of faith in Thee. Fortify my soul in its weak places by Thy grace and Spirit that I may crown Thee Lord of my life. Thou knowest that I love Thee. Calm my restless spirit and help me to sense Thy nearness at all times. I ask it in Thy name. Amen.

❧ ❧ ❧

11. O Christ, teach me Thy patience that I may be strong when discouragement hovers near. May the vision of God break anew with the coming of each new day, and may all the day be radiant with the benediction of Thy presence. Give ear to my prayer, for Thy name's sake. Amen.

❧ ❧ ❧

12. Heavenly Father, I pray Thee to make this a bright and joyous day. May I be kept from lingering under overhanging clouds of doubt and gloom. Let me have the full joy of living in the sunshine of Thy love. May my soul be filled with the sweet anticipation of that immortal hope that should be the abiding possession of all Thy children. I ask it in the name of Jesus my Saviour. Amen.

❧ ❧ ❧

13. O God, save me from the sin of hypocrisy and pretense. Grant that no zeal for religious forms or niceties may be mistaken for zeal for Thee. Forbid that my profession of religion should be incompatible with its expression in my daily life. Hear my prayer, O Lord, for Jesus' sake. Amen.

❧ ❧ ❧

14. Almighty God, I need Thee and Thy guidance amid the perplexities of life. Help me to be conscious of Thy presence through the day. Give me strength and wisdom and courage to meet the responsibilities of this day. Life is

hopeless without Thee. Oh! how I need Thee in my daily walk! Forgive my sins, for Jesus' sake. Amen.

    ❧ ❧ ❧

15. Most gracious God, I worship and adore Thee. My all I surrender into Thy hands of love. Guide me through this day, and may I never cease to make Thy will my own. In every changing scene of life's uncertain way, I trust Thee and pray that Thou wouldst lead me on. In the name of Thy dear Son, I pray. Amen.

    ❧ ❧ ❧

16. O God, I pray Thee accept the dedication of my life to Thee, and may I walk daily in the assurance of certain victory through Jesus Christ, who is the same yesterday, today, and forever. He has faced every test and trial that life can offer and has passed through it all unscathed. May this knowledge inspire me to press forward to the higher heights of Christian experience with a courage that can know no defeat. I pray in His blessed name. Amen.

    ❧ ❧ ❧

17. O Lord, I come to Thee for health and guidance in this day's responsibilities. Grant, I beseech Thee, all needed strength and quicken my devotion to Thee, that I may serve Thee in an acceptable manner. Grant that I may be kept safe in body, soul, and spirit; through Jesus Christ my Lord. Amen.

    ❧ ❧ ❧

18. O God, reveal Thyself to me through the sacred pages of Thy Holy Word, through the life and teachings of Jesus, and through the experiences of prayer. I crave a deep sense of Thy reality and covet every privilege that leads to a more vital knowledge of Thee. Until I really know Thee, my heart is restless and cries out as did Thy servant of old,

"Oh that I knew where I might find him! that I might come even to his seat!" In Christ's name. Amen.

❧ ❧ ❧

19. I love Thy Word, O God. May it be a fountain of living water to my soul. May I get fresh blessing, fresh manna, fresh life from its study every day. May I have the strength and the vision to sink shafts down into this mine of eternal truth, for its possession is more precious than silver and gold; its promises keep life radiant with hope; its living messages transform the dry and barren wastes of life into green and growing fields of experience. Lead me into a deeper knowledge of it, for Jesus' sake. Amen.

❧ ❧ ❧

20. O God, Thou art my fortress and defender. Preserve me from the enemies of my soul. Give me valor and constancy that I may fight a good fight against those perils which may beset my path today. Banish from me, I beseech Thee, unworthy fear and help me to live in the atmosphere of Thy perfect love; through Jesus Christ the Lord. Amen.

❧ ❧ ❧

21. Heavenly Father, keep alive in my soul the hope of a world wherein mankind may dwell together in brotherhood and fullness of life. The secret of the good life lies at the very heart of the redemptive message of the Gospel. Hasten, O Lord, the realization of the ideal of the Kingdom of God on earth, as expounded by Jesus Christ. May a passion for a realization of this ideal draw men together in united effort, for His name's sake. Amen.

❧ ❧ ❧

22. Heavenly Father, deliver me from the spirit of avarice and undue anxiety. Grant that no passion for earthly pos-

sessions may ever dull my spiritual perception or turn my mind away from Thee. Give me a confident dependence upon Thy fatherly care and teach me to seek first the things Thou dost require. In Christ's name. Amen.

🍀 🍀 🍀

23. My Father, teach me that Thou art limited in the bestowal of Thy gifts in my life only by the measure of my asking. Help me to ask largely that I may receive largely. Innumerable times I limit Thy giving because I do not ask according to Thy ability to give. The fountains and streams of Thy love are overflowing for me. Heaven's windows are waiting to be opened to pour Thy blessings into my life. O come, gracious God, and flood my heart with Thy immeasurable grace. For the sake of Thy Son, my Saviour and Master. Amen.

🍀 🍀 🍀

24. O glorious Christ who art the express image of the Father, deepen within my soul the impress of Thy Spirit, that I, too, may bear likeness to the Father. Thou art the bright and morning Star, the Lily of the Valley, the One altogether lovely in whom the Father dwelt that He might reconcile the world unto Himself. Take up Thy abode within my soul, that I may know the sweetness of Thy presence, and grow more like unto it. Show forth Thy glory in my daily life; for Thy name's sake. Amen.

🍀 🍀 🍀

25. Heavenly Father, I lift my voice today with millions of others throughout the world in gratitude for the gift of Thy Son, Jesus Christ. In His incarnation Thy glory is revealed, and all the beauty and perfection of Thy divine nature manifested. I thank Thee for all the spiritual riches He has brought into the world, as a gift from Thee. May this day symbolize in a very real way the dawning of a day

of peace and good will among men. In the blessed name of Christ, my Redeemer. Amen.

ॐ ॐ ॐ

26. Heavenly Father, hasten the day when the kingdoms of this world shall become the Kingdom of the Lord Jesus Christ. May this rebellious world come under the rule of Him on whose shoulders Thou hast placed the redemption of the world. Continually manifest Thyself, O God, in the midst of men, and grant that the light of Thy holiness may dispel the dark forces of evil. I pray Thee, give us a vision of a new world wherein dwelleth righteousness, justice, and good will. In Christ's name. Amen.

ॐ ॐ ॐ

27. Blessed Lord, I pray Thee to give my soul a real sense of peace and security. Still the storms that beset it. May it find satisfaction by reposing in Thy love and enjoying the assurance that my sins have been blotted out. O pilot this frail bark of mine over the tempestuous seas and bring it safely into the harbor at last. In Thy name. Amen.

ॐ ॐ ॐ

28. O Christ, Thou hast blazed a way through all the doubts and uncertainties of life, through all the sin and wretchedness of the world. That way leads up to the very throne of God. With an assurance that goes to the heart of humanity's need, Thou hast said: "I am the way, the truth, and the life." Give me that way to know and that life to live; for Thy blessed name's sake. Amen.

ॐ ॐ ॐ

29. O Christ, Thou who wast content to have Thy crown of glory fashioned in agony, Thou who didst suffer that Thou mightest gather the glorious harvest of a world redeemed, forbid that I should ever shrink from following in

Thy steps—even though it be the way of the cross. Deliver me from pettiness, and enable me to breathe the atmosphere of eternity in my daily walk. In Thy name. Amen.

❧ ❧ ❧

30. Almighty God, as I approach the close of the year, I can truly say with the psalmist, "Thou crownest the year with thy goodness." There has been no irksome pressure in my daily work, because Thou hast been a constant presence. Thou hast been with me in the hour of trial. Thou hast shared my anxieties and sorrows. Thou hast sustained me daily with Thy love and care. "Thou crownest the year with Thy goodness," and unto Thee I give all praise; through the Lord Jesus Christ. Amen.

❧ ❧ ❧

31. O God, Thou hast been gracious to me during the year that is past, and I am thankful. Thou hast filled the days with tokens of Thy loving-kindness and renewed my soul with a sense of Thy presence. Grant that this commerce with Thee may strengthen and equip me to meet the duties that confront me in the new year ahead, through Jesus Christ. Amen.